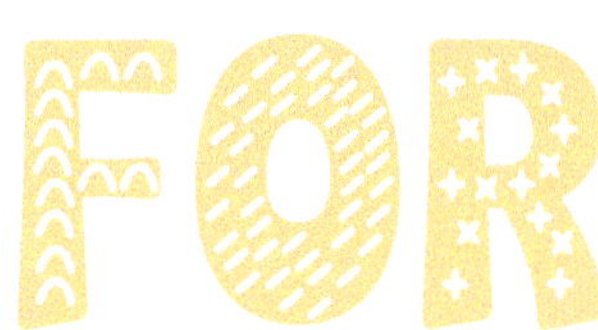
CRAFTS
FOR
KIDS

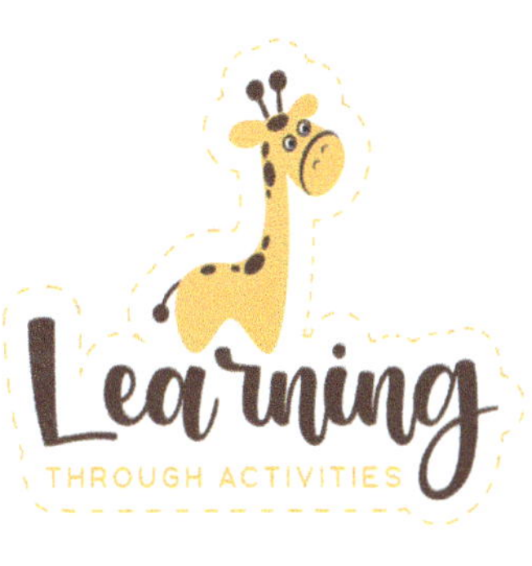
Learning
THROUGH ACTIVITIES

SPECIAL BONUS!

Want These 2 Books For <u>FREE</u>?

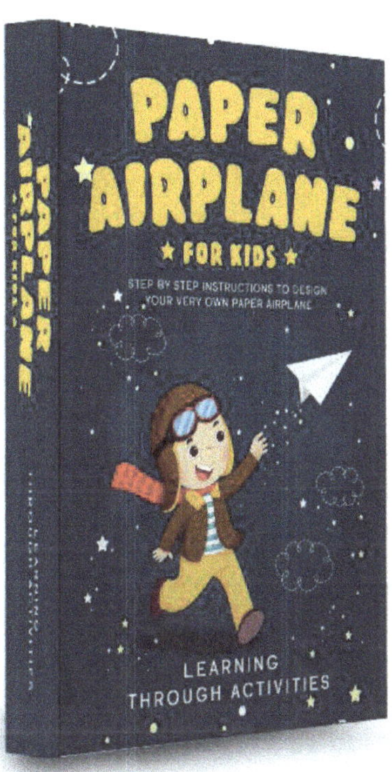

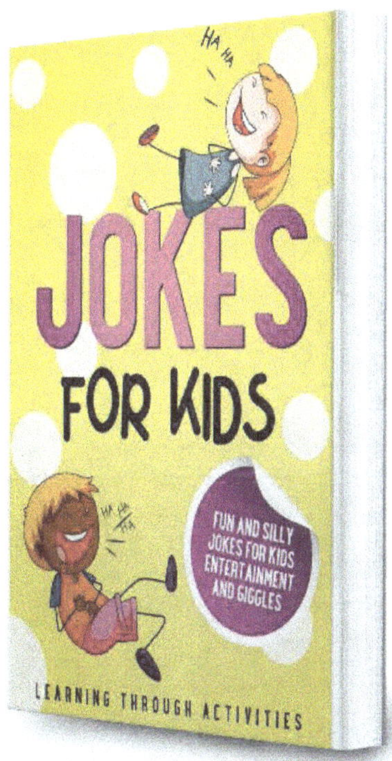

Get **<u>FREE</u>**, unlimited access to these and all of our new kids books by joining our community!

Scan W/ Your Camera To Join!

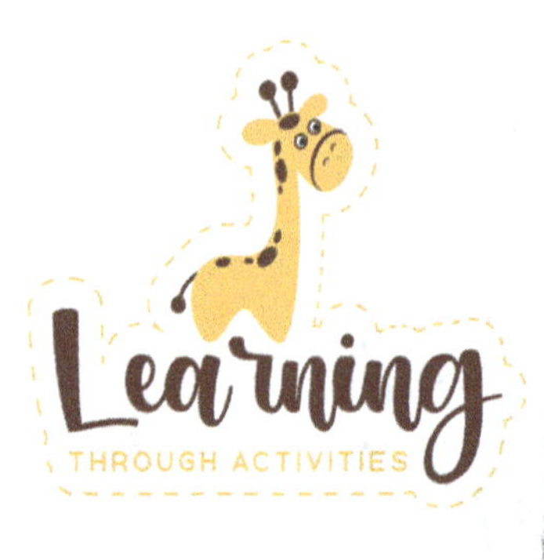

CONTENTS

PAPER ROLL STAMPS...4

FOAM STAMPS...5

SPLASH PAINTING...6

PET ROCK..7

GEOMETRIC ANIMALS...8

LEAF PRINTING...9

FOAM PRINTMAKING...10

DINOSAUR HANDS...11

SUNCATCHER...12

FINGER PUPPETS...14

BUILDING BLOCK BOX...15

MANDALA STONES...16

SCRATCH ART..17

LEAF FAIRY...18

CRAYON BUTTERFLY...20

HUNDREDS, TENS AND ONES..21

MR. GRASS..22

GREATER THAN, LESS THAN, EQUAL TO................................24

KERPLUNK...25

CARTON BOAT..26

PAPER SPINNER..27

BOOKMARKS..28

WALKING WATER..30

FAIRY JAR..31

POPSICKLE TREE...32

WINDMILL...34

FISHING CUPS...36

MY PLACE IN THE WORLD..38

FRIENDSHIP BRACELET..40

BUNNY..42

CHALK POPS...44

LEAF DREAM CATCHER...45

ROBOT HAND...46

SOLAR SYSTEM...48

PYRAMID PUZZLE...50

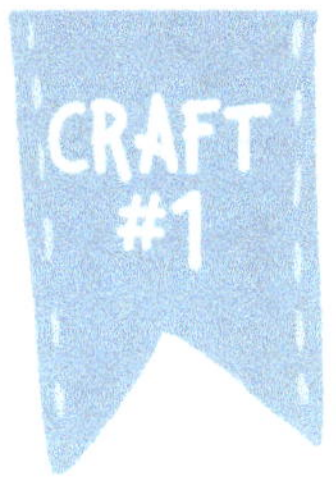

PAPER ROLL STAMPS

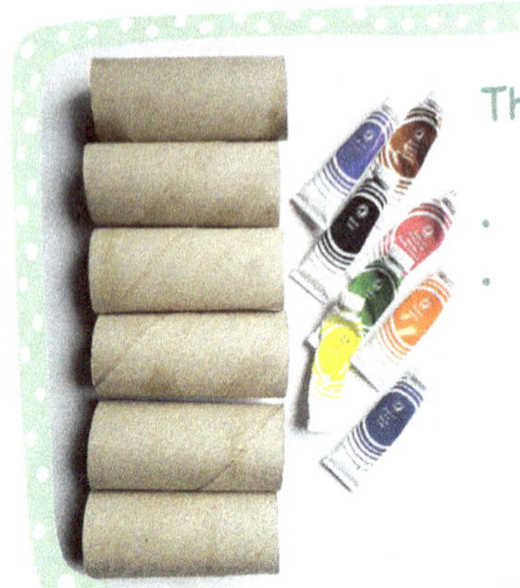

This is what we'll need:

- Toilet paper rolls.
- Paint.

Something that we all have at home, and that we can easily upcycle, are toilet paper rolls. These days we are going to do some crafts to turn them into entertaining games and art supplies. Let's start by making some stamps with geometric shapes.

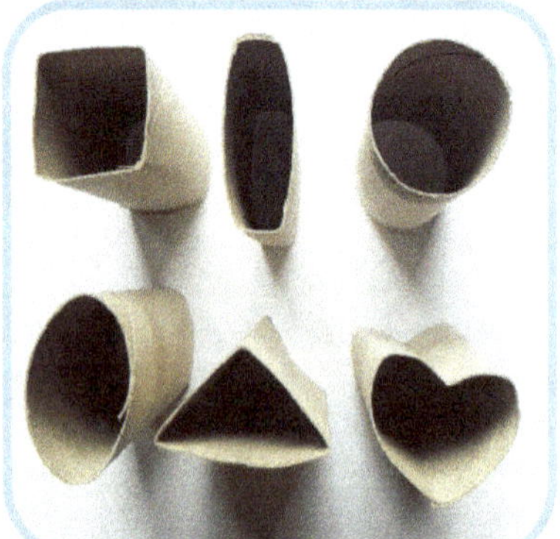

Step 1. Fold the paper rolls to give them our favorite geometric shape. We are going to shape them into a triangle, square, rectangle, heart, oval, and leave a round one as it is.

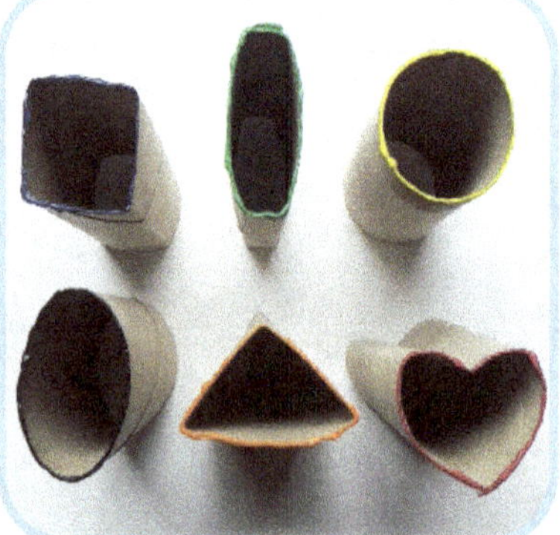

Step 2. Dip them in paint.

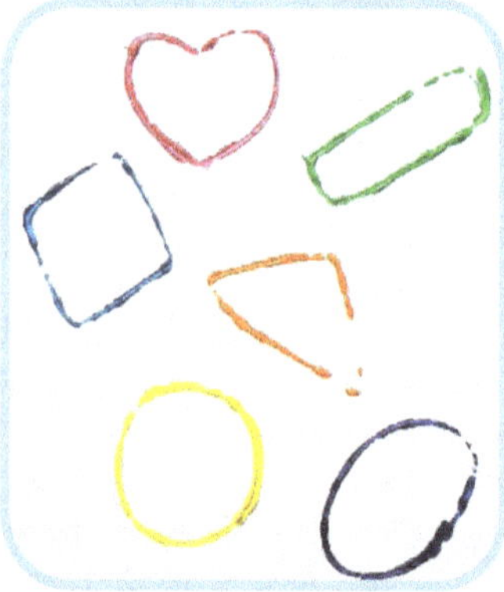

Step 3. Let's create works of art!

Tip: We can use several paper rolls, cut and glue them together, to make more complex stamps, like flowers or letters.

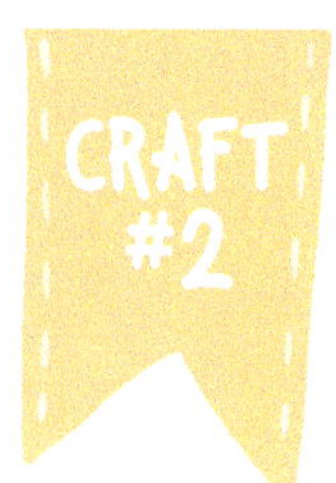

FOAM STAMPS

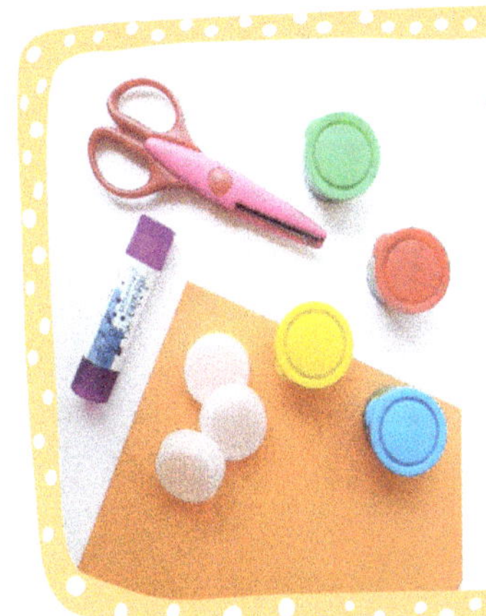

This is what we'll need:

- Foam.
- Bottle caps.
- Scissors.
- Glue.
- Paint.

Drawing with stamps is not only super fun for kids of all ages, but it helps the little ones to develop fine motor skills that will help them later in their process of learning to write. We can make our own stamps with very few materials, would you like to see how?

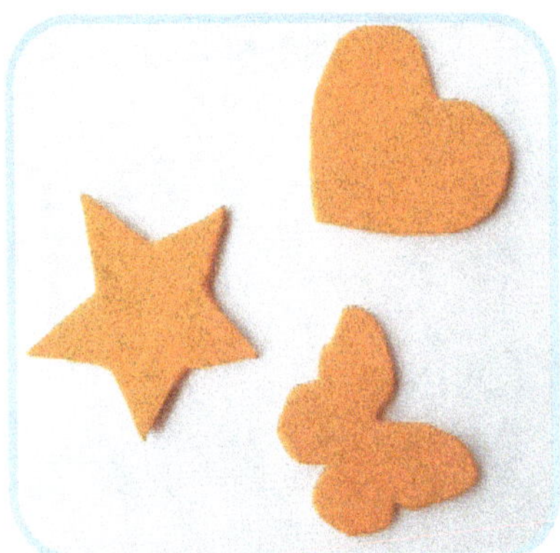

Step 1. Cut out all the foam shapes that we want.

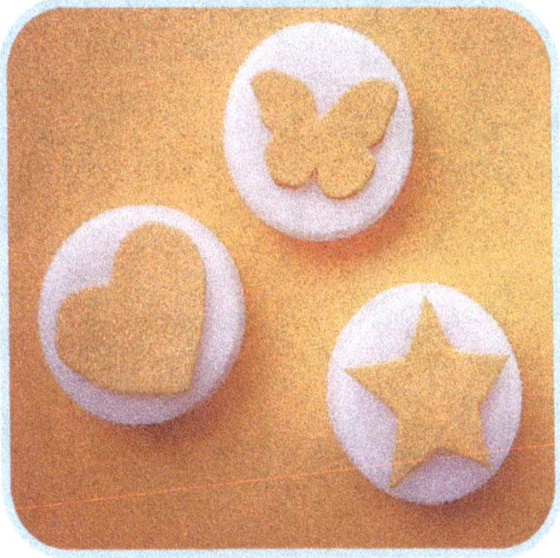

Step 2. Glue each shape to the outside of a bottle cap.

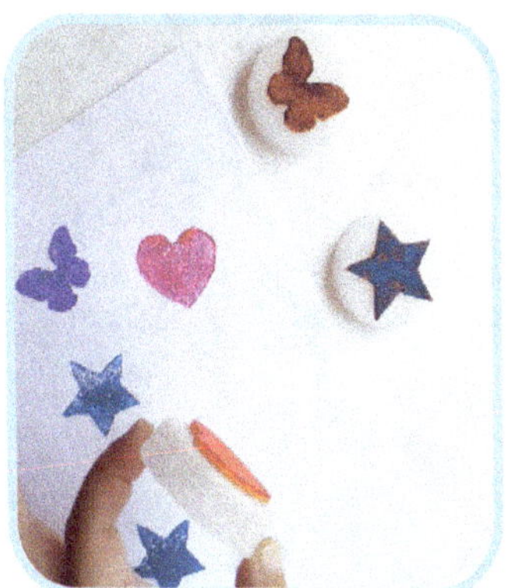

Step 3. Dip the stamps in some paint and create works of art!

Tip: If the foam we're using is too thin, we can cut out the same shape several times and glue them together to make it thicker.

SPLASH PAINTING

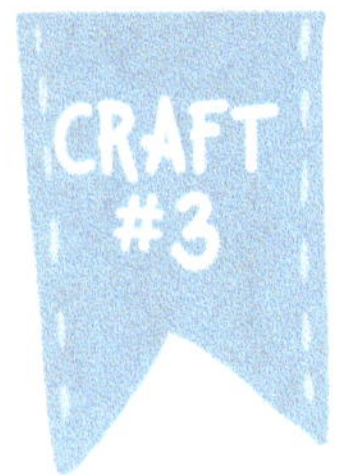

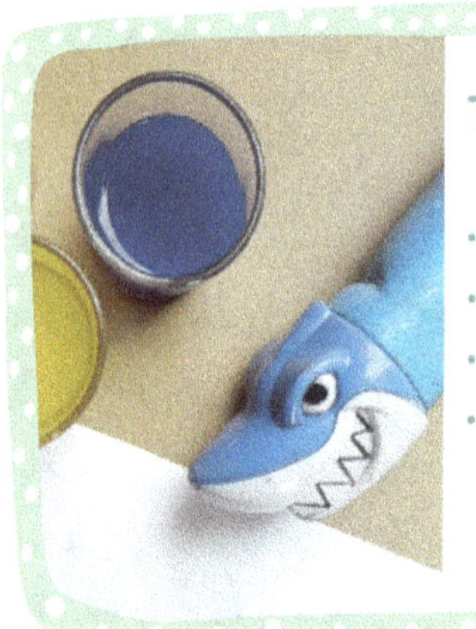

This is what we'll need:

- Paper sheet.
- Liquid paint.
- Thumbtack or tape.
- Water gun.

Do your kids get bored during summer break? Not anymore! With today's craft we will turn any boring moment into a work of art.

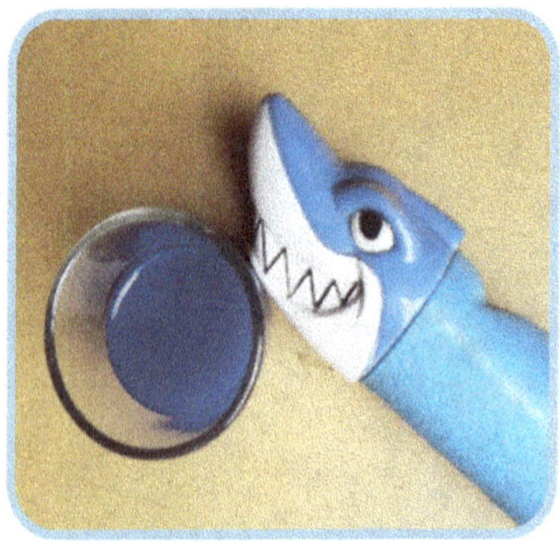

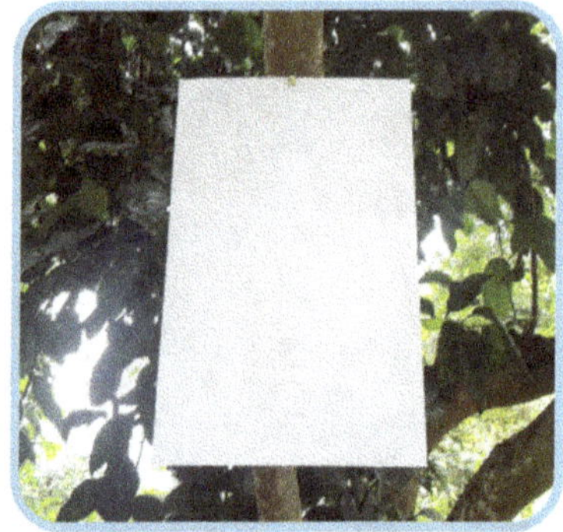

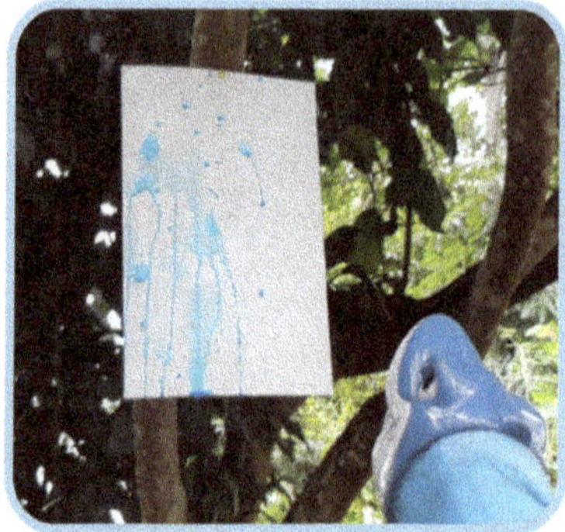

Step 1. Fill one or more water guns with liquid paint. If we don't have liquid paint, we can mix acrylic paint and water.

Step 2. Attach the sheet of paper, preferably white, to a wall that can get dirty, a tree or, if we have one, an easel.

Step 3. Let's become painters for a bit! Shoot the gun on the paper to create our splash of art.

PET ROCK

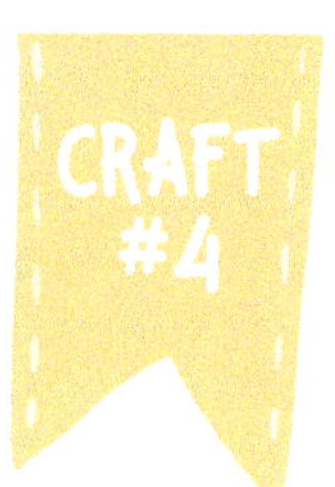

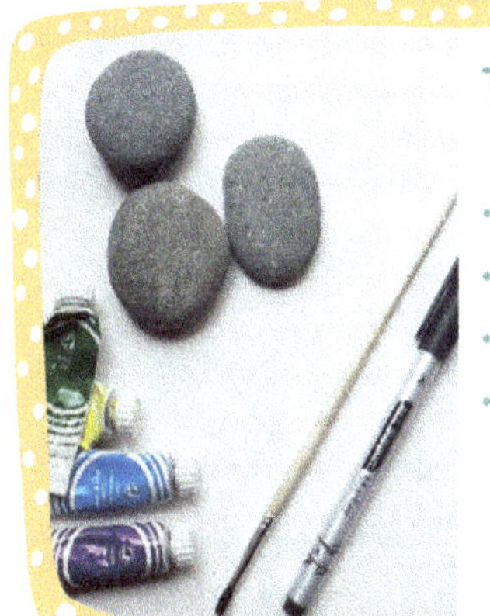

This is what we'll need:

- Rocks
- Paint and brush.
- Black permanent marker.
- Optional: googly eyes.

Pet rocks are so much fun and a great excuse to take a long walk outside and enjoy nature while we search for the perfect rocks. You already have them?

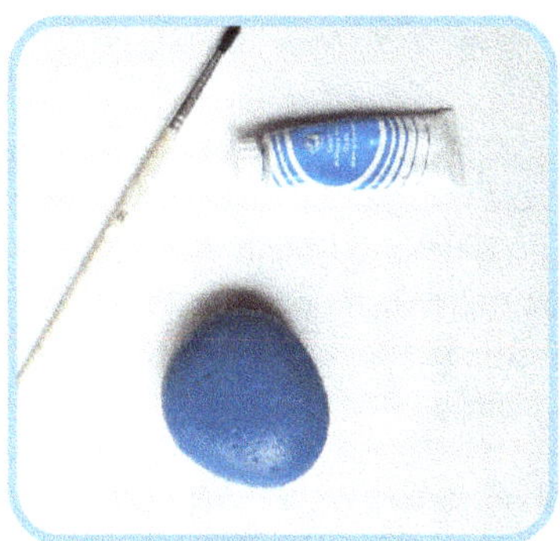

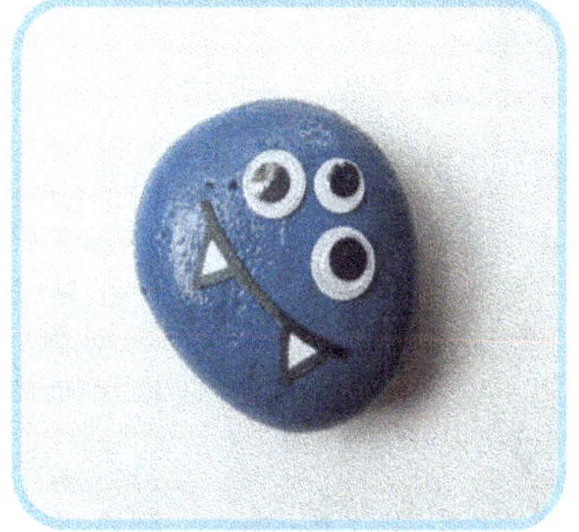

Step 1. Paint the rock in the color or colors we've chosen and let the paint dry well.

Step 2. Paint details like the eyes or teeth, and outline them with a black permanent marker. We can also draw them on paper and glue them, or use googly eyes.

Tip: We can add hair using wool, cardboard wings, or legs made with pipe cleaners, whatever we can think of!

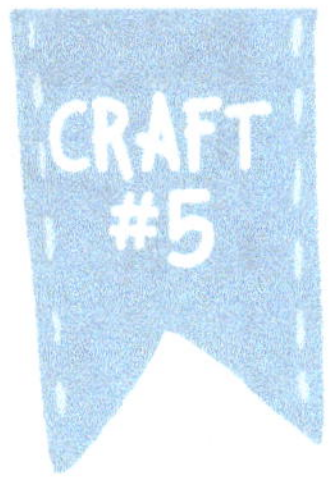

GEOMETRIC ANIMALS

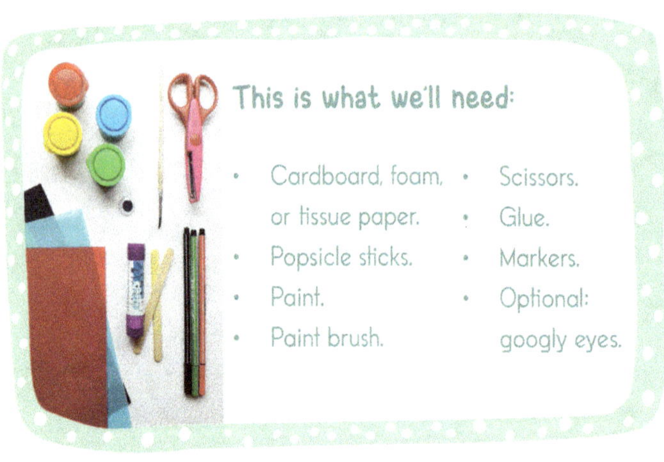

Learning to identify geometric shapes correctly is very important, since they directly affect the development of other skills, such as reading or writing. The first step to learn letters, numbers, symbols... is to recognize their shape. Learning geometric figures can be much more fun with these little animals that we are about to make!

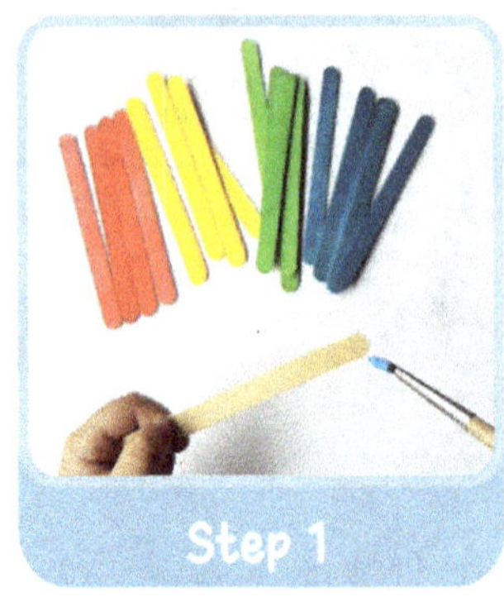

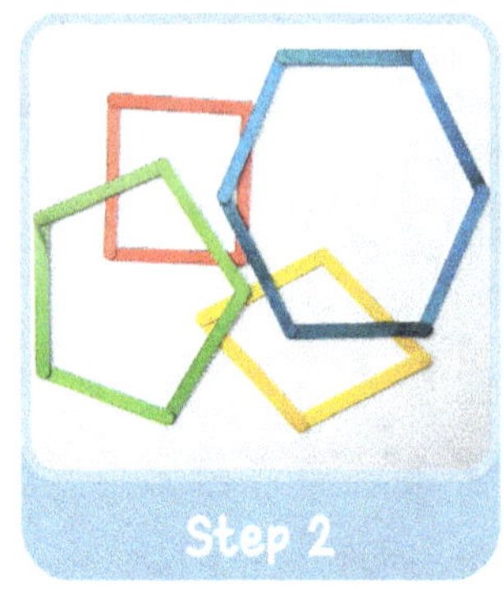

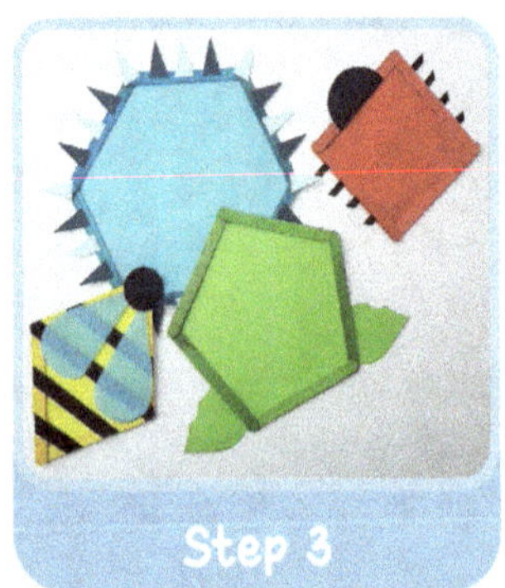

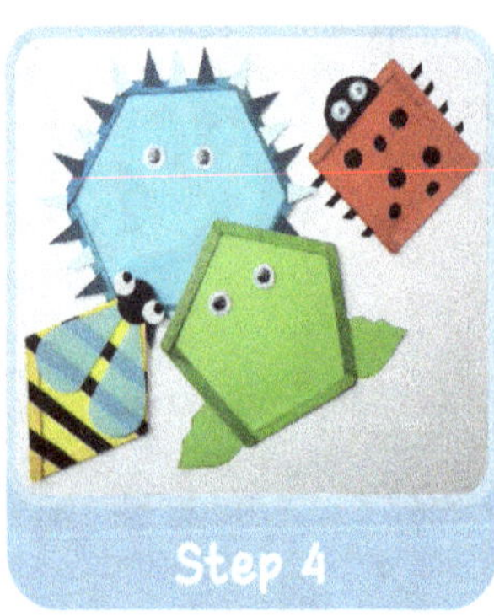

Step 1. First, we need to paint the popsicle sticks in the colors we are going to need. Since we are making a diamond bee, a pentagon frog, a hexagon puffer fish and a square ladybird, we're painting 4 yellow, 5 green, 6 blue and 4 red sticks.

Step 2. Let the paint dry, and then form the geometric shapes with the sticks, and glue them together. We'll end up with a yellow diamond, a green pentagon, a blue hexagon, and a red square.

Step 3. To make our animal's bodies, legs, and wings, we cut pieces of cardboard, foam, or tissue paper (we used all of them so you can see how they look, but you can choose your favorite), and glue them to the shapes we just made.

Step 4. Finally, we glue their eyes, and use markers to draw some details.

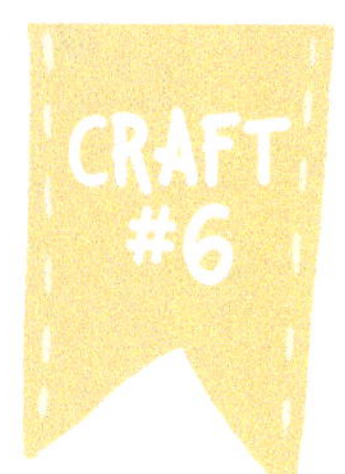

LEAF PRINTING

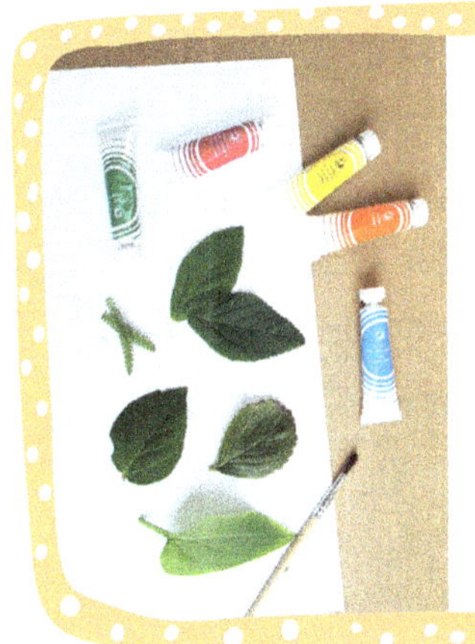

This is what we'll need:

- Leaves.
- Paint and brush.
- Black or white cardstock.

We can take advantage of the leaves falling from the trees during the fall to take a walk and collect some of them to make amazing crafts. Here we have a very easy one to do.

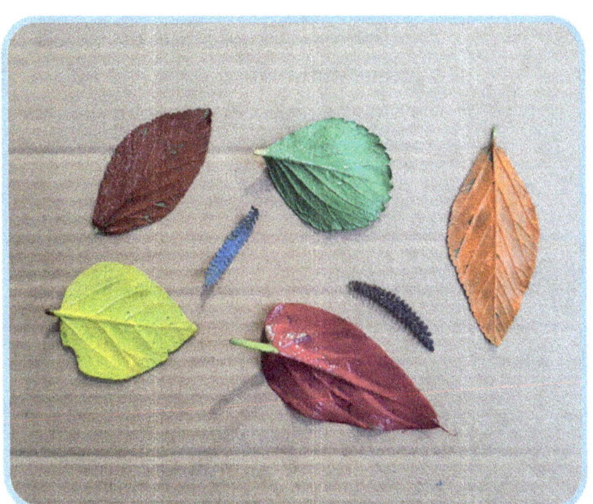

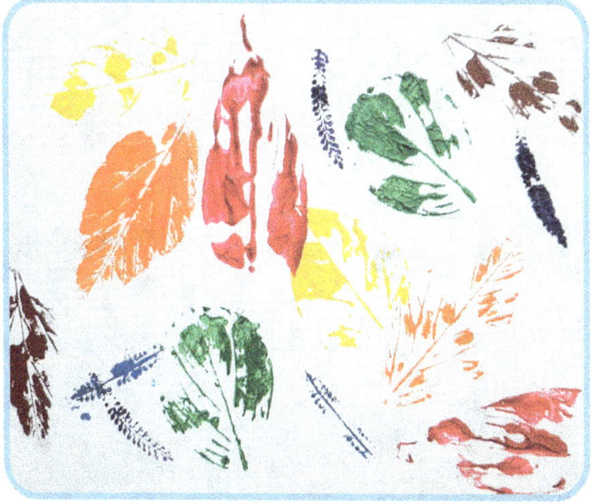

Step 1. Cover the back of the leaves with a thin, even coat of paint. We cover the back because it's the part with the most texture.

Step 2. Press each leaf firmly against the black or white cardstock to leave their impression. If we paint each leaf a different color or using a certain palette, we'll get some beautiful works of art.

Tip: We can also use crayons, just put the leaves facing down under a thin paper sheet instead of cardstock and rub the crayons over each leaf.

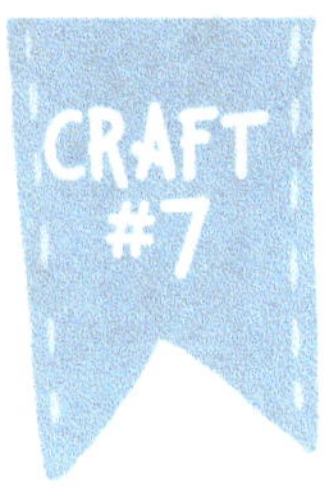

FOAM PRINTMAKING

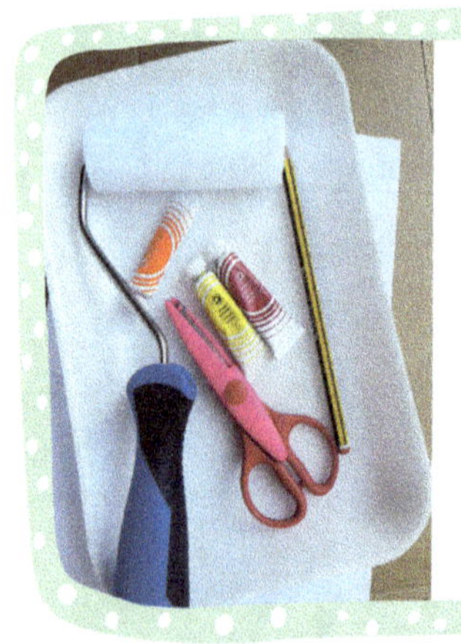

This is what we'll need:

- Foam plate.
- Paper or cardstock.
- Paint.
- Scissors or cutter.
- Brush or roller.
- Pencil, stick or skewer.

Have you ever tried the art of printmaking? It's so fun and easy if we have a foam plate or tray at home that we don't need. The result is amazing, but the best part is that we can use each design many times!

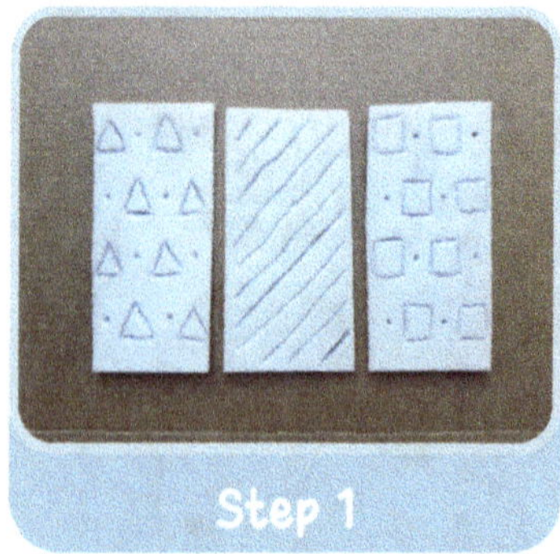

Step 1

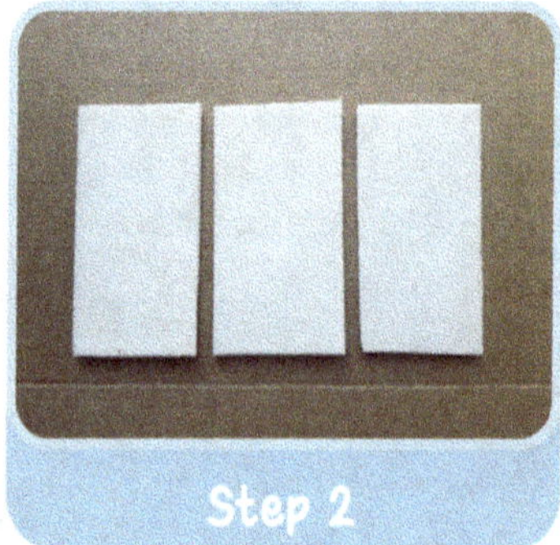

Step 2

Step 1. Cut out the bottom of the foam plate or tray to make a flat rectangle. We can also cut it in any other shape depending on our design.

Step 2. Use a pencil, stick, or skewer to draw on the foam piece. Press hard enough so that the lines in the drawing are a bit deep.

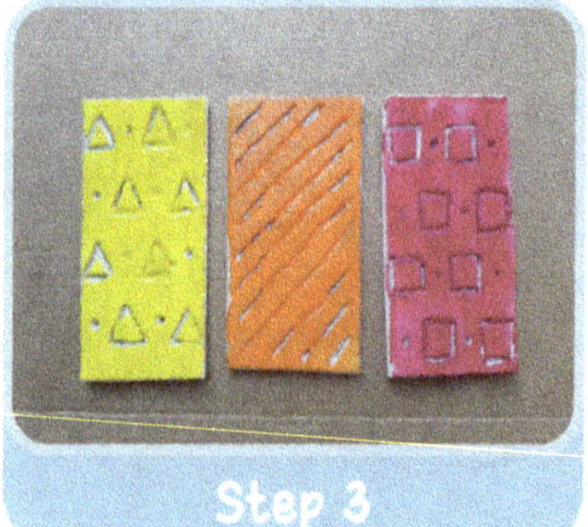

Step 3

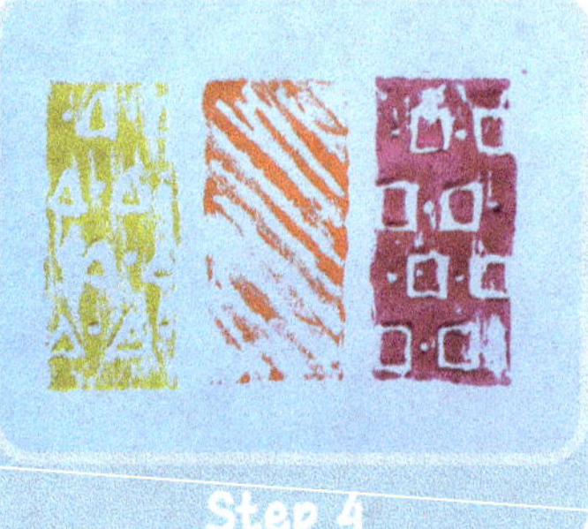

Step 4

Step 3. Spread a thin coat of paint over the foam piece using a brush or roller. We can use one or many colors, that's up to us.

Step 4. Lightly press the foam piece for a few seconds on a sheet of paper or cardstock to transfer our design. Separate them and let dry.

Tip: We can use this technique to make beautiful Christmas, birthday, or any other celebration cards.

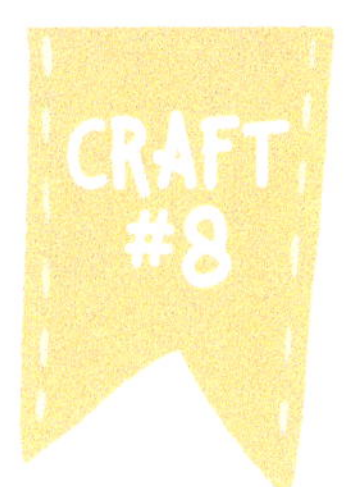

DINOSAUR HANDS

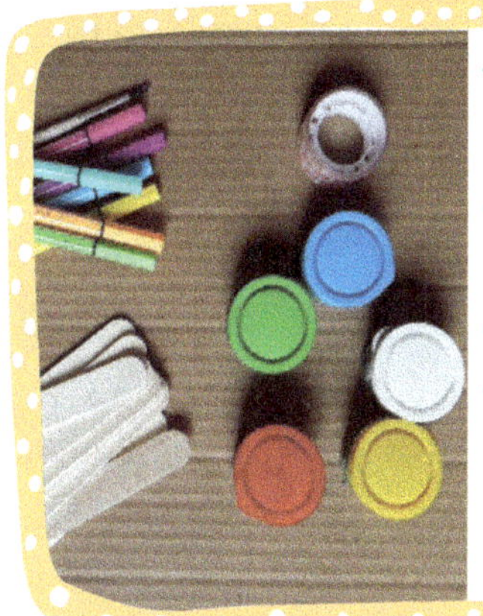

This is what we'll need:

- Popsicle sticks or tongue depressors.
- Tape.
- Markers, paint and brush.

Fact: kids love dinosaurs. Wait until they discover they've had one in the palm of their hand all this time with this fun craft!

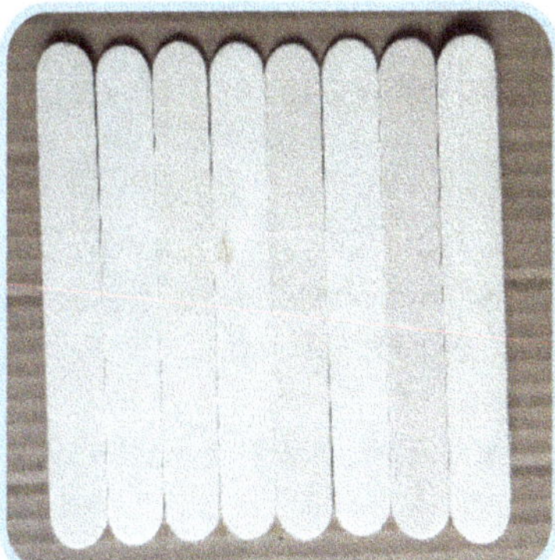

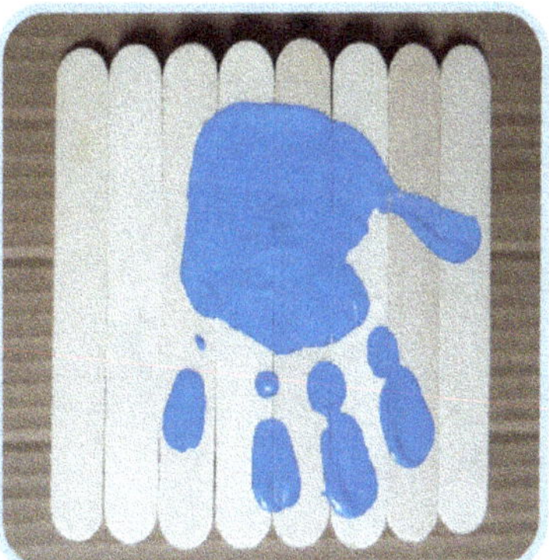

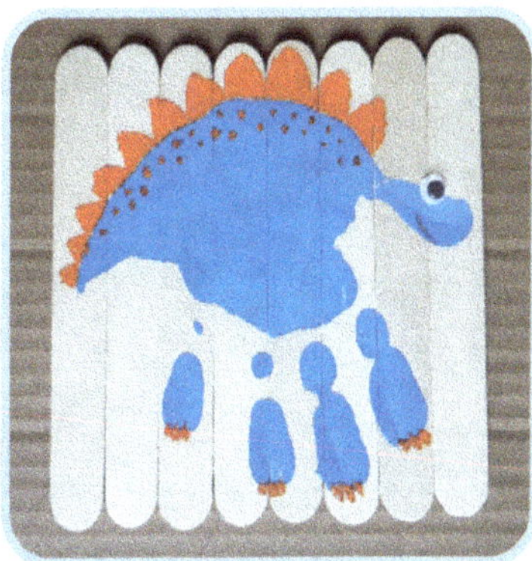

Step 1. Place popsicle sticks or tongue depressors side by side until they are about the size of our child's hand, then tape them together.

Step 2. Flip the popsicle sticks or depressors over so that the tape is at the back. Time to dip our hands in our favorite paint and leave our handprint on the front of the sticks!

Step 3. As we only have 5 fingers, we will need to add the tail or the head of the dinosaur. After that, decorate as we like using brushes and different markers for the details, we can even add some googly eyes to make it more fun!

Tip: Once finished, we can leave it as it is and use it to decorate our kids' room or we can, for example, remove the tape from the back and mess up the pieces to let them solve the puzzle.

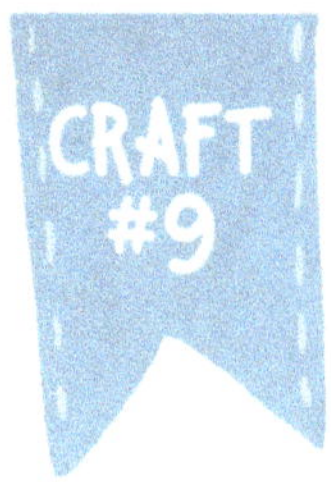

SUNCATCHER

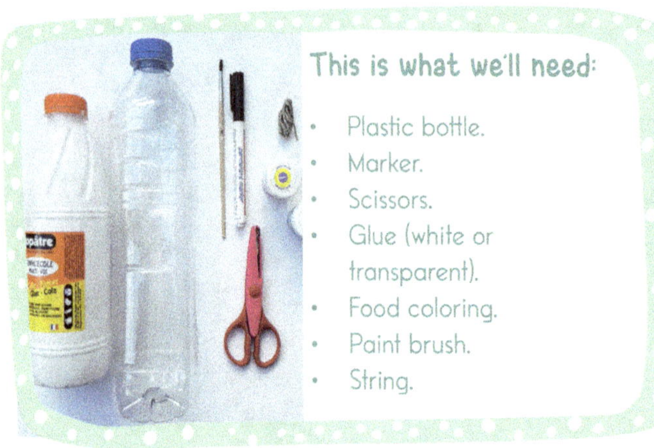

Suncatchers are ornaments that catch sunlight, creating beautiful, colorful patterns. They are said to bring harmony if they are made with love. Let's put a lot of love, and creativity, into this craft!

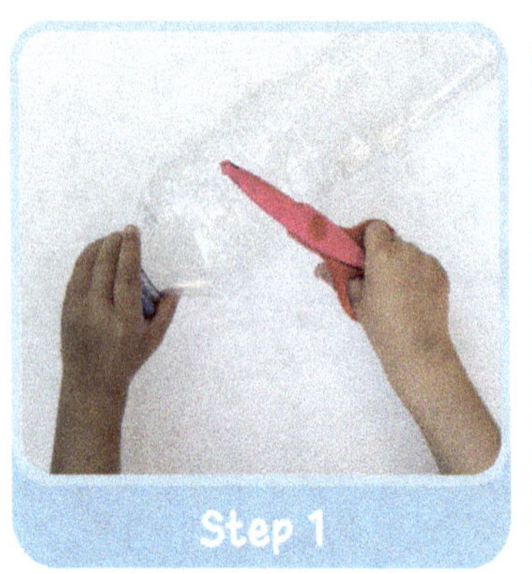

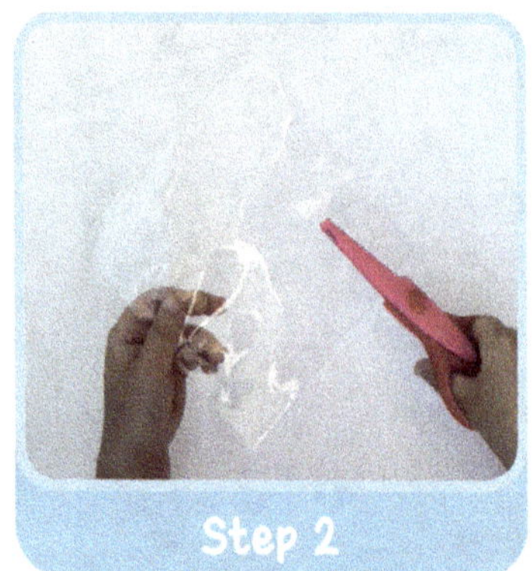

Step 1. Cut the top and bottom of the plastic bottle and keep just the middle section.

Step 2. Cut that piece vertically, so that we end up with a square or rectangular plastic sheet.

Step 3. Now we have to place our kid's hand on the plastic sheet and trace its outline with a marker.

Step 4. We cut out the silhouette with the scissors.

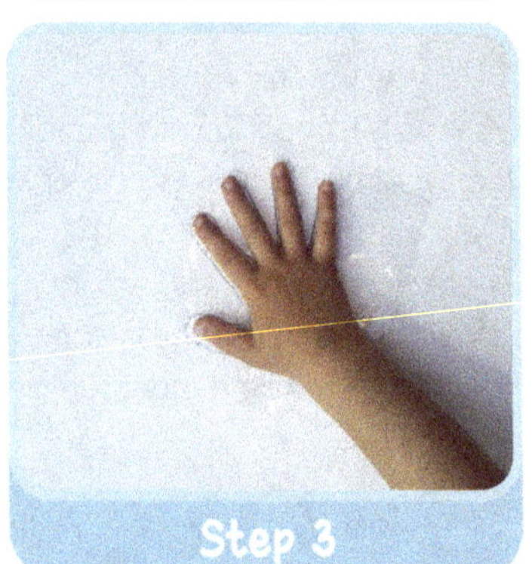

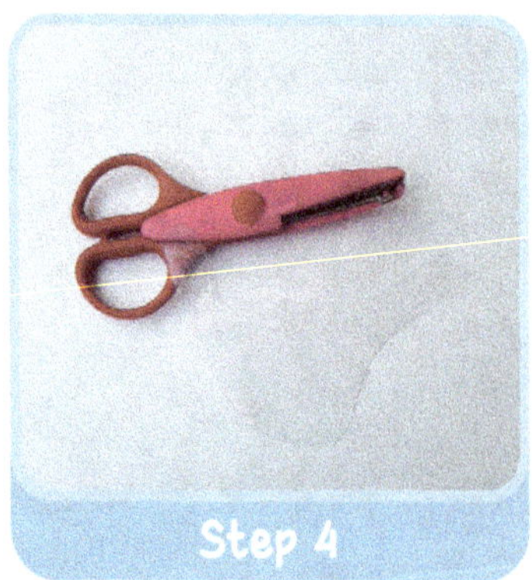

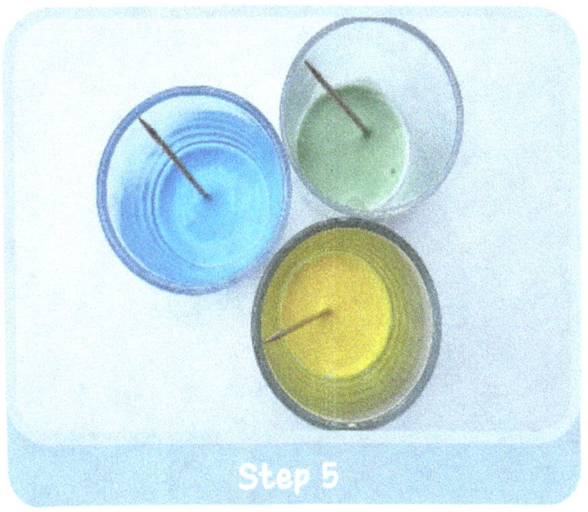

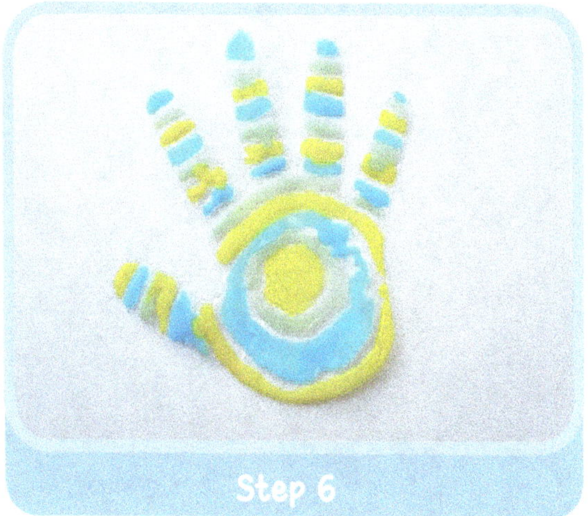

Step 5

Step 6

Step 5. To make our special suncatcher paint we need to mix one tablespoon of school glue with 2-3 drops of food coloring. We can use white glue, but transparent glue works best.

Step 6. Once we have mixed all the colors we need, we can let our creativity fly and paint the suncatcher in the way we like the most.

Step 7. After the paint is dry, we make a small hole in our suncatcher so we can put a string on it and hang it where everyone can see it.

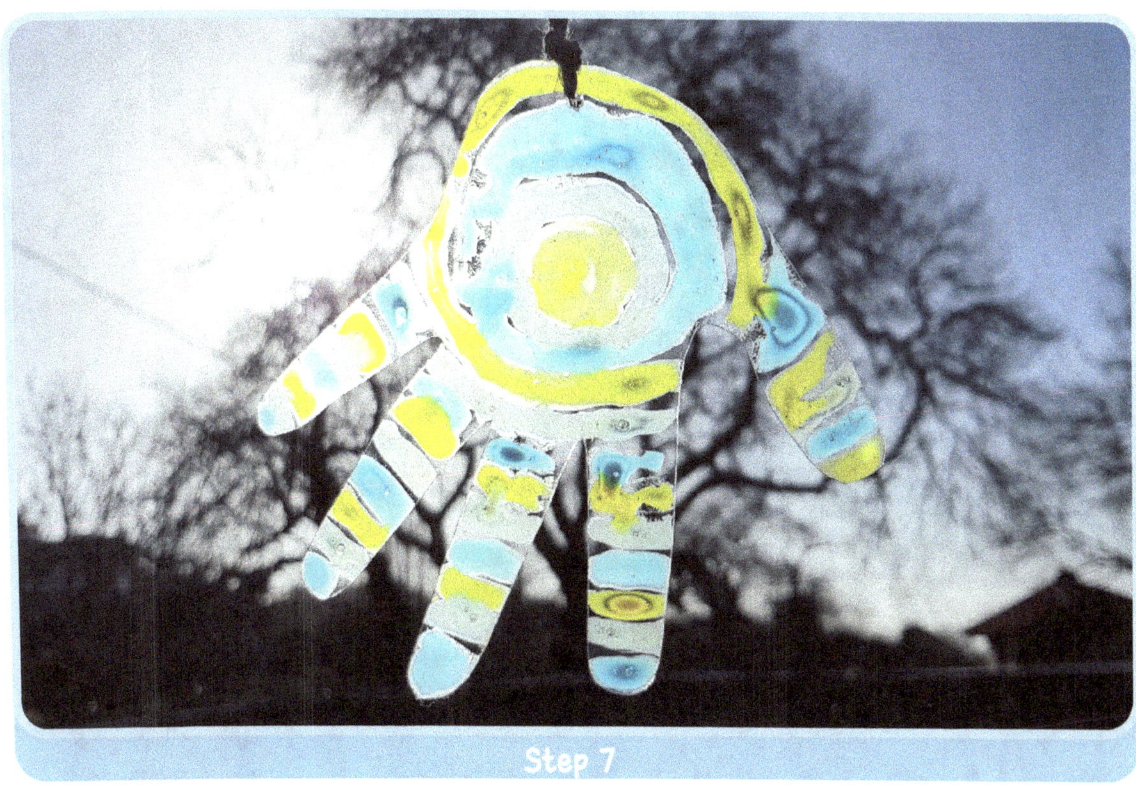

Step 7

Tip. We can get creative and make any shape and size that we want, even connect several suncatchers to make a more complex one.

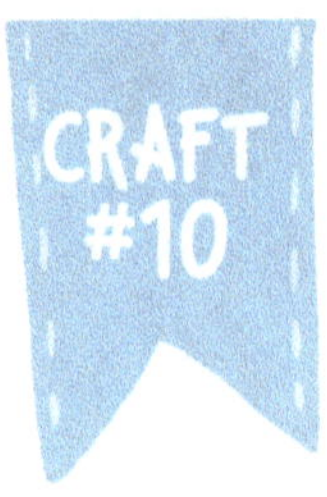

FINGER PUPPETS

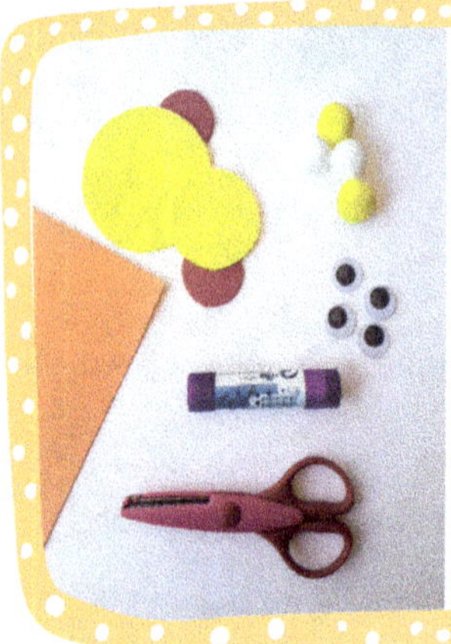

This is what we'll need:

- Cardboard or foam.
- Googly eyes.
- Pompoms.
- Scissors.
- Glue.

A great idea to get our little ones to like reading is to tell stories with the whole family. And there is no more fun way to tell a story than with... Puppets! How about we make a few finger puppets?

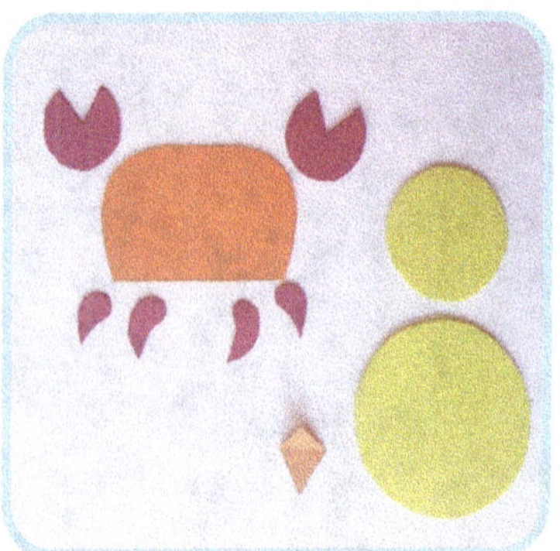

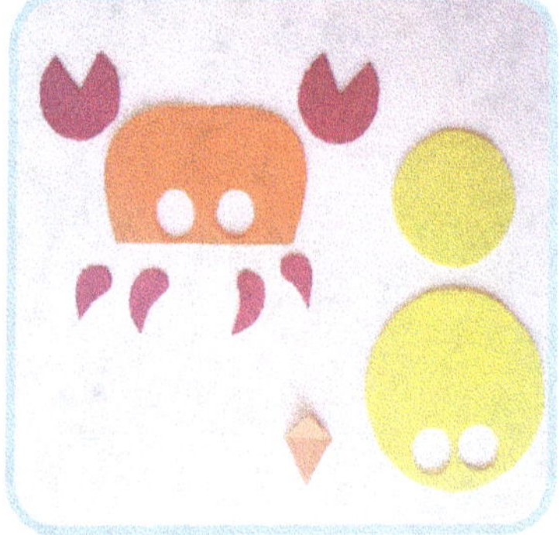

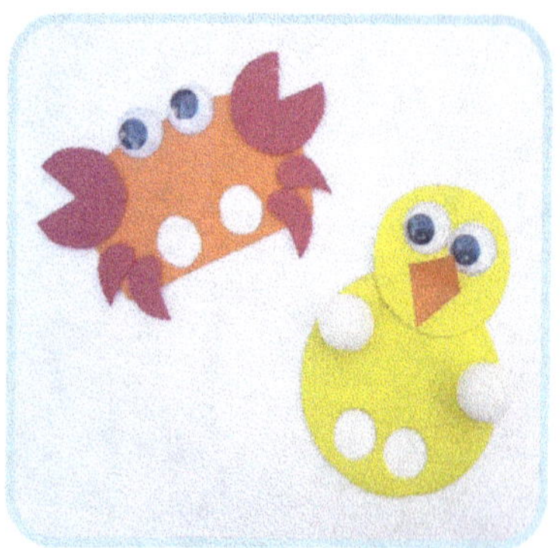

Step 1. The first thing we have to do is choose the animal that we are going to make, and then draw its parts on the cardboard, and cut them out. In this case we have chosen a chick and a crab.

Step 2. In the lower part of the body, we make the two holes where our fingers will go.

Step 3. We glue all the pieces together, including the eyes and that's it!

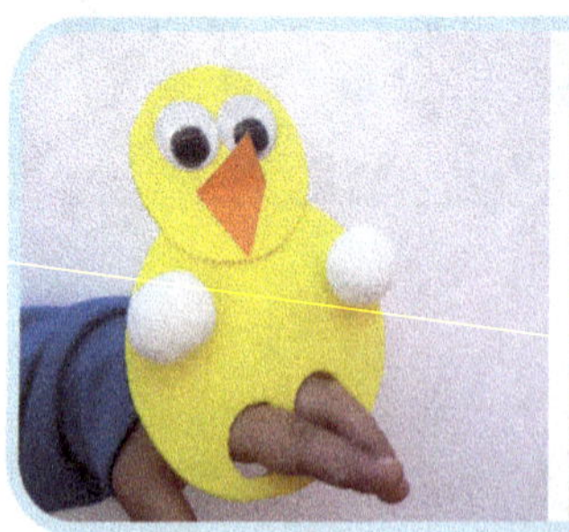

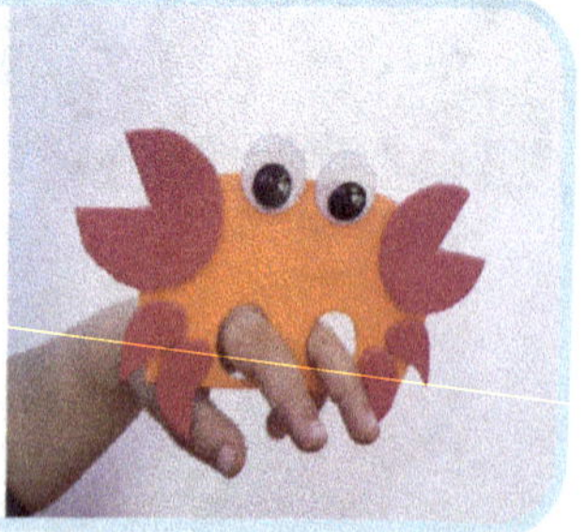

BUILDING BLOCK BOX

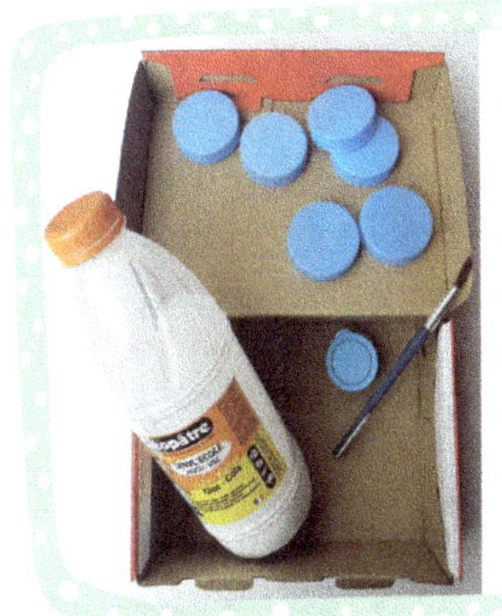

This is what we'll need:

- Shoe box.
- Plastic bottle caps.
- Glue.
- Paint.
- Paintbrush.

Kids love building blocks, they are fun, colorful, and allow them to express themselves freely. I bet more than one of us have stepped on a block that has been left on the floor, right? How about we make a really cool, giant block to store them all?

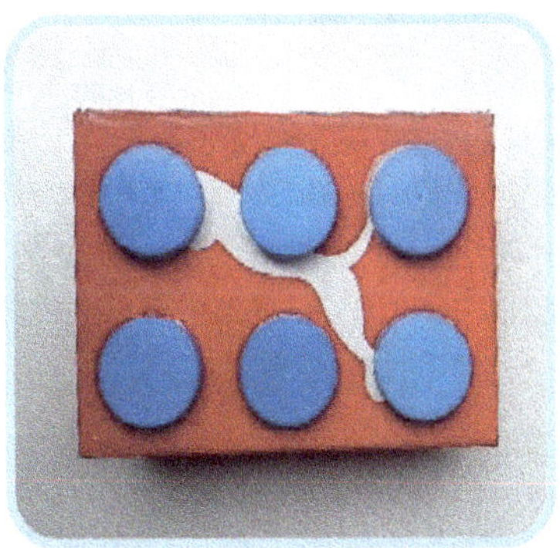

Step 1. Decide where you want to place the bottle caps and glue them to the empty shoe box. The exact number of caps will depend on the size of the box; here we have a small one, so we used just six caps.

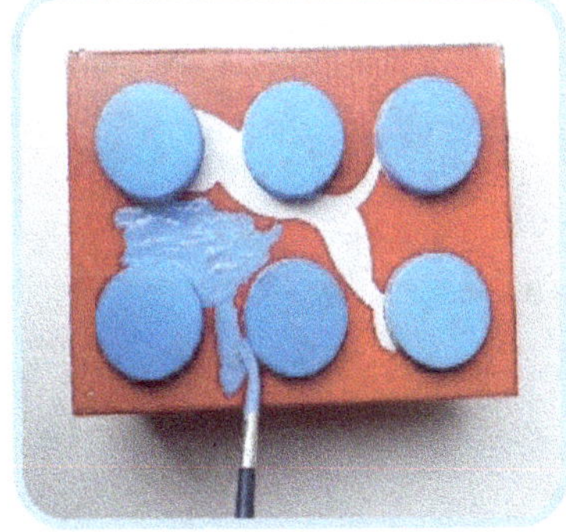

Step 2. Paint everything with your favorite color and let it dry.

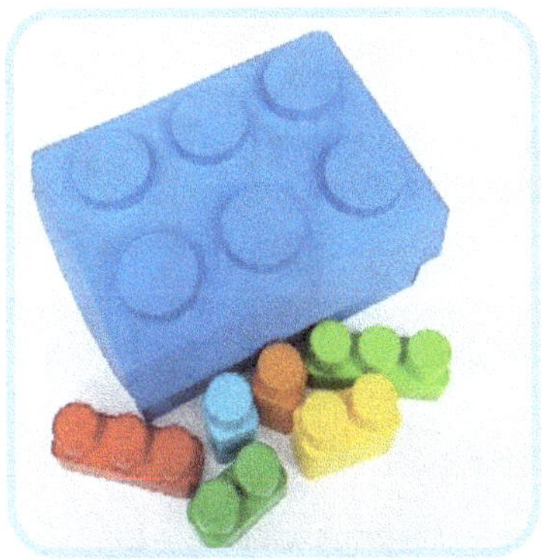

Tip: If we don't have enough bottle caps or they aren't big enough, we can use cut-out plastic/paper cup bottoms.

MANDALA STONES

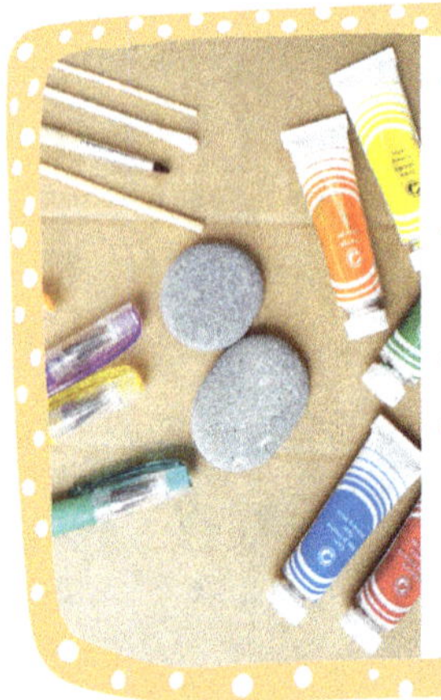

This is what we'll need:

- Stones (flat and with a smooth surface).
- Paint, pens, and/or markers.
- Brushes or tools of different sizes (toothpicks, cotton swabs, skewers...).

Today we're going to make a beautiful, colorful craft that's also a great way to improve our kids' fine motor skills and their patience (and ours too!).

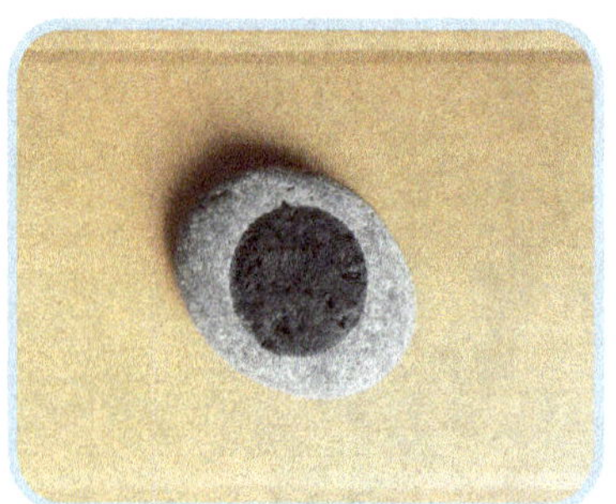

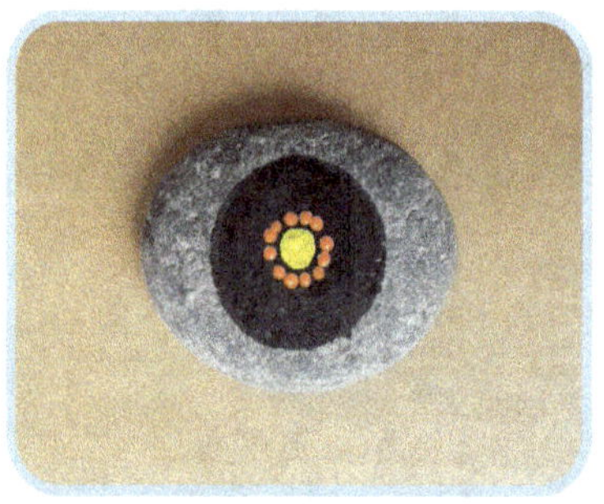

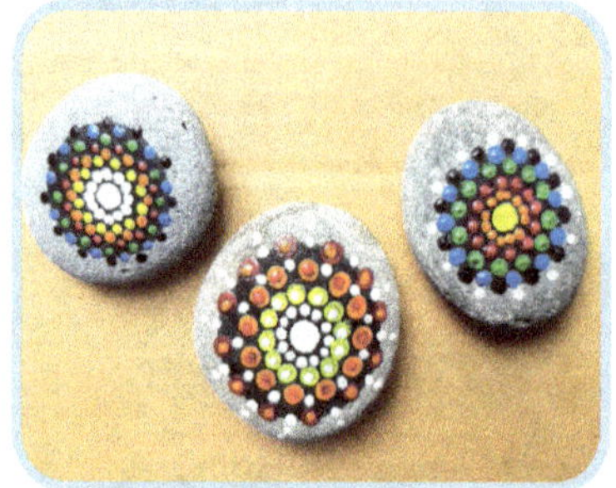

Step 1. Paint a black circle in the center of the stone using either paint or a black marker. Leave some space around the edges unpainted. This will make the colors pop, but it's totally optional.

Step 2. With the thickest brush or tool, paint a circle in the center of the stone. Then, for example, make tiny dots around it using a smaller brush or tool.

Step 3. Keep making concentric circles of dots up to the edge of the black circle or as far as we want if we didn't paint one. We can make all the dots the same size, some larger than others, larger dots in each circle... And if there are any, fill in the gaps between the larger dots with tiny dots using a color that stands out.

Remember that this is a kids' craft and it will probably not turn out well on the first try, so this is a good opportunity to help our kids manage their frustration and expectations too. Don't worry, practice makes perfect!

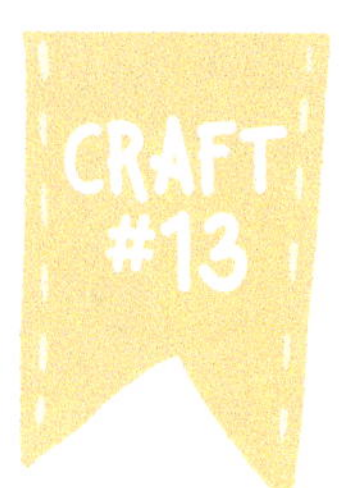

SCRATCH ART

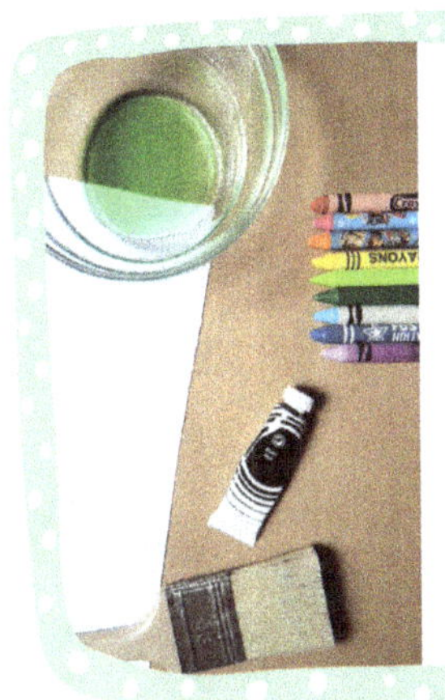

This is what we'll need:

- Black paint.
- Brush.
- Oil pastels.
- Dish soap.
- Small bowl.
- White cardboard.
- Popsicle stick or skewer.

Have you ever tried scratch art? It's super fun and so easy to do at home.

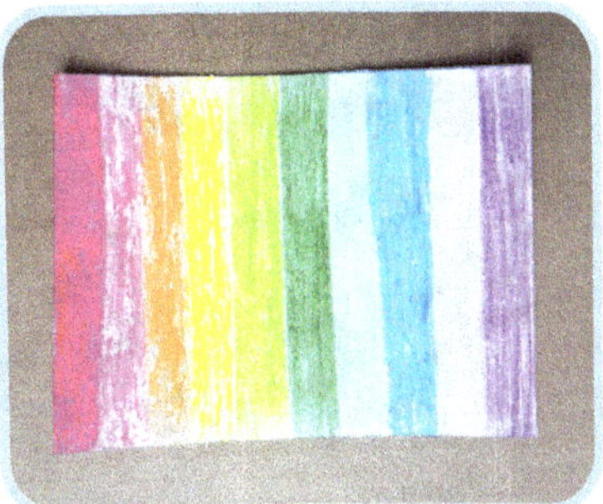

Step 1. Color all the white cardboard with oil pastels, making sure to press hard so that everything is well saturated. We can paint it as we like, we chose to make a rainbow.

Step 2. In a small bowl, mix black paint with a little dish soap, this will make the paint stick better to the oil pastels, and let it dry well. Try to keep the paint layer a bit thick, but it's okay if there is some color showing underneath.

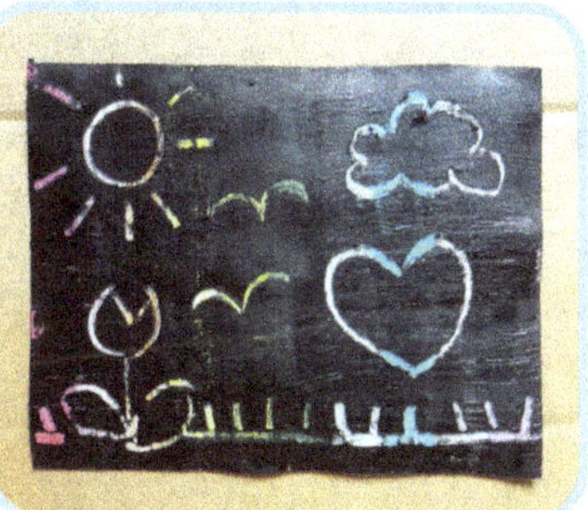

Step 3. Using a popsicle stick or a skewer, scratch the black paint carefully and we'll see how all the colors show to give life to our drawing.

Tip: If we use a popsicle stick we can experiment with its different sides to make thicker or thinner lines, or use different tools to make lines of different thickness.

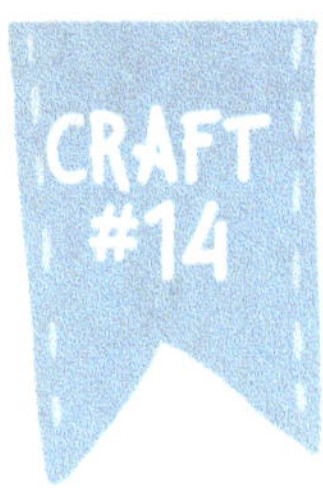

LEAF FAIRY

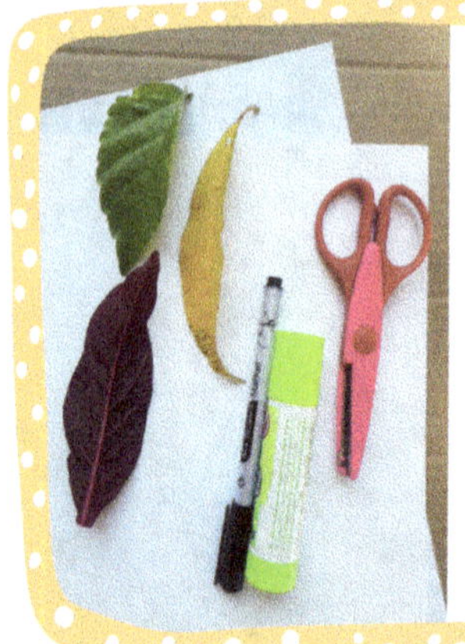

This is what we'll need:

- Leaves.
- Cardstock.
- Glue.
- Scissors.
- Markers.

Do you believe in fairies? Have you ever seen one? Well today is the day! Let's go for a walk and collect different colored leaves for this cute craft.

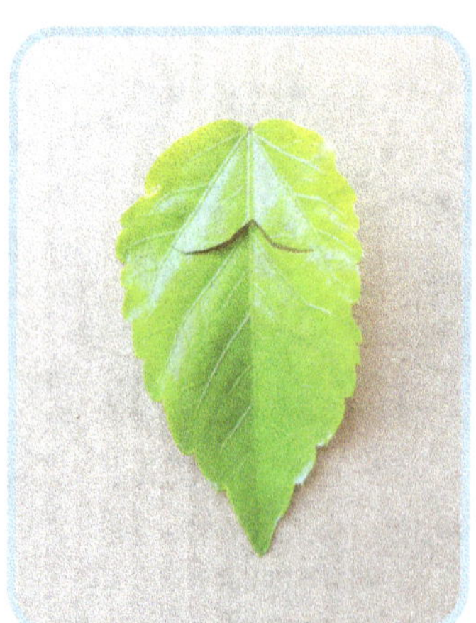

Step 1. Take a leaf, fold it in half, and make a curved cut in its upper half to create the hairline.

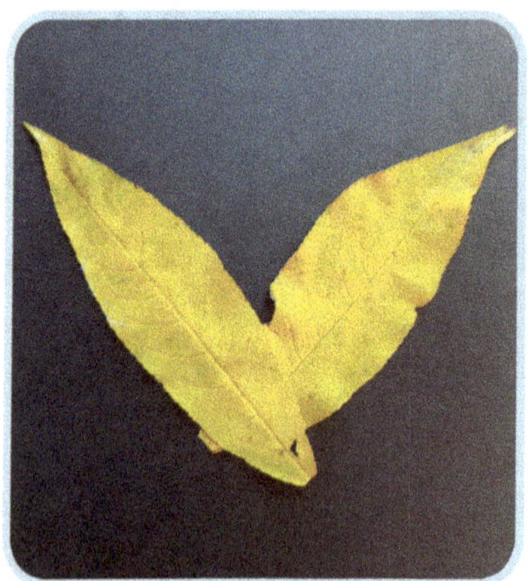

Step 2. Use 2 leaves of another color to make the wings and glue them to a cardstock sheet.

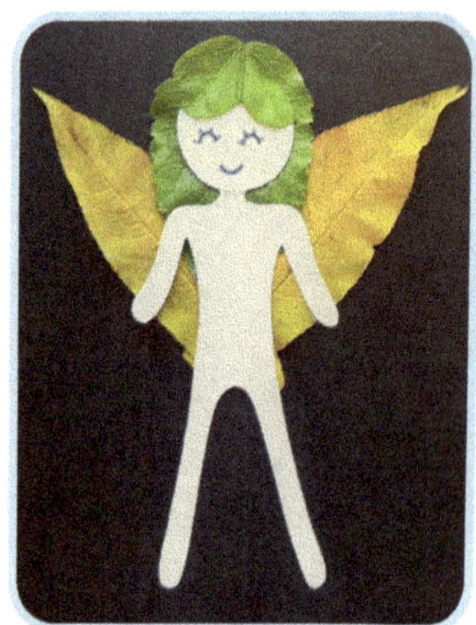

Step 3. Cut out the fairy's body and draw her face with a marker, insert the head on the leaf from the first step and glue everything on top of the wings.

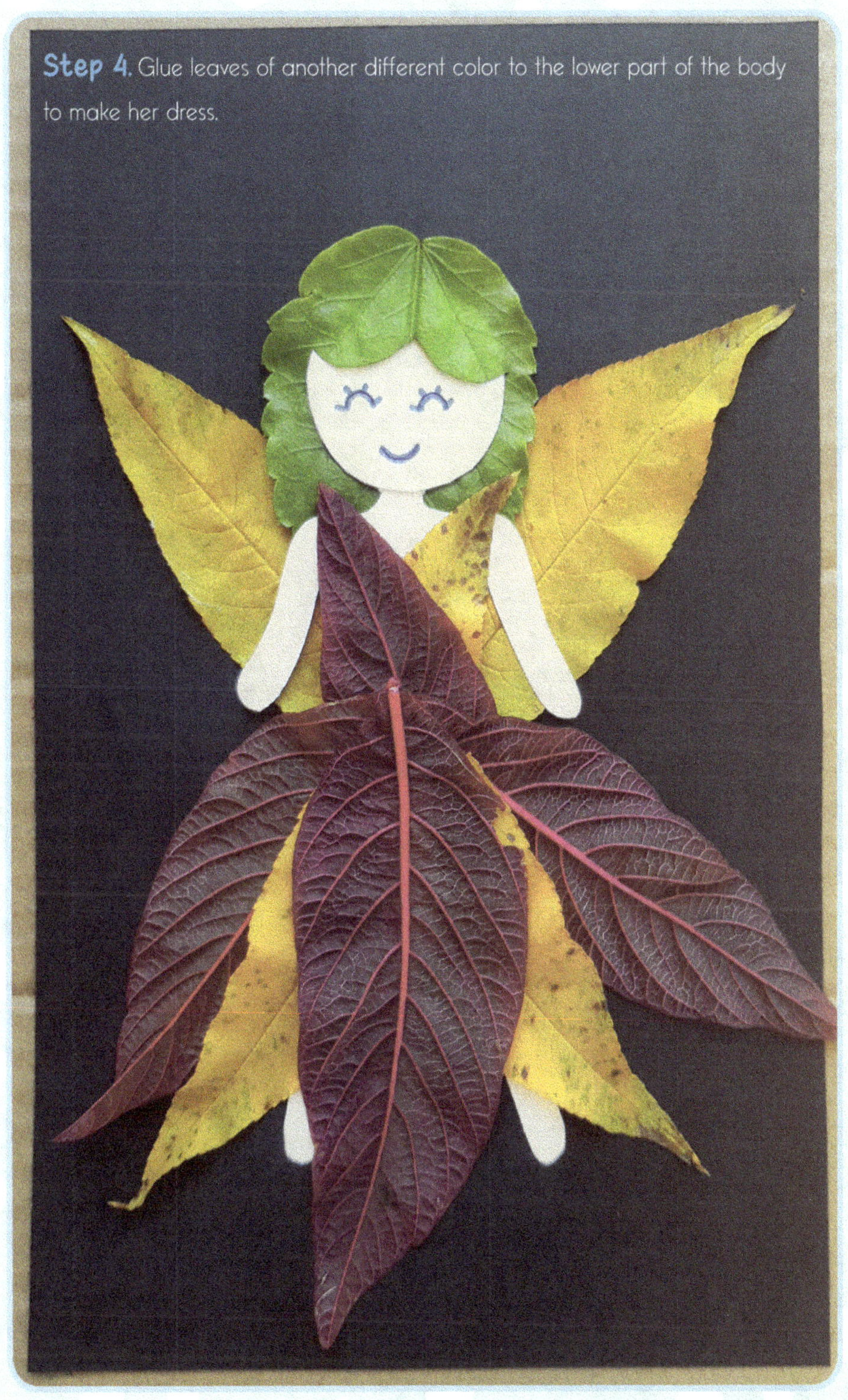

Now we can add other details if we want, such as a headband or a flower in her hair.

CRAYON BUTTERFLY

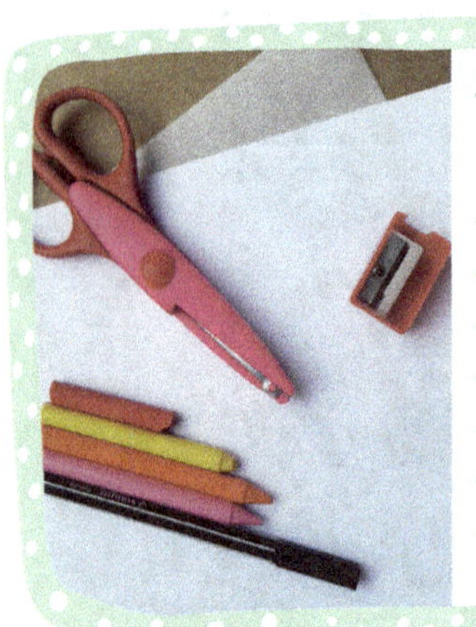

This is what we'll need:

- Paper.
- Marker.
- Crayons.
- Scissors.
- Pencil sharpener.
- Parchment paper.
- Iron (not pictured).

Do you have pieces and pieces of crayons that you don't know what to do with? Here's a great idea!

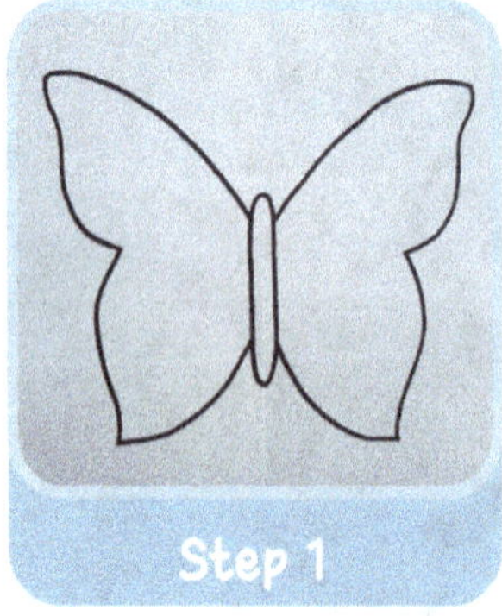

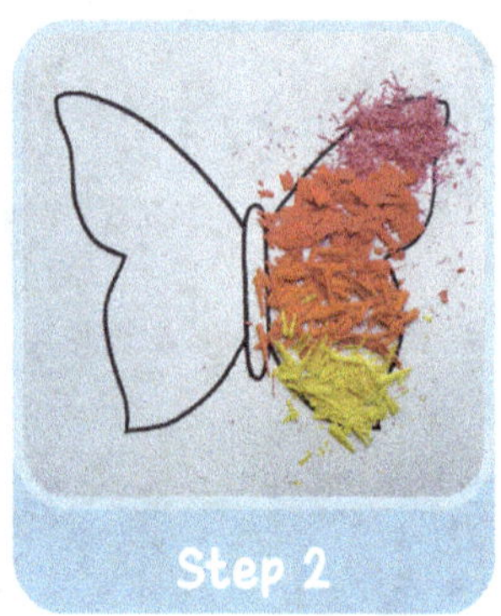

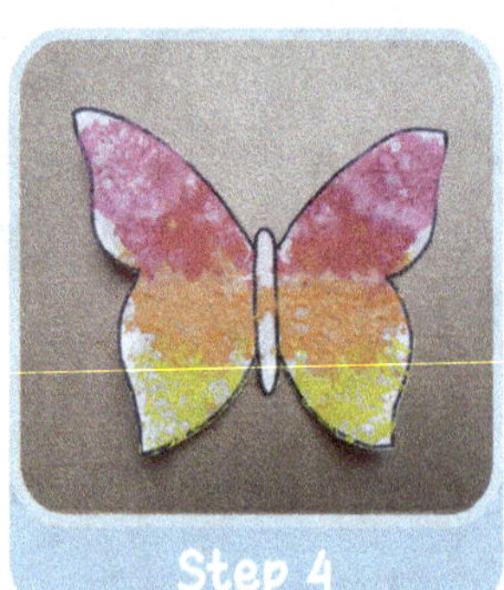

Step 1. Take a marker and make your favorite drawing on a piece of white paper, we made a butterfly. Fold the drawing in half and then unfold it.

Step 2. Use a sharpener to get crayon shavings and place them on top of the drawing in whatever order we want, although the result is better if the adjacent colors are similar. We need to cover just half the drawing.

Step 3. Once we're done with the shavings, fold the drawing in half, cover it with parchment paper, and press it with the iron. Set the iron to its minimum, press the drawing for 1-2 seconds, and repeat until the shavings are completely melted.

Step 4. Unfold the design, wait for it to dry well and cut it out.

Tip: We can also make designs that don't need lines or are more abstract, such as rainbows or trees.

HUNDREDS, TENS AND ONES

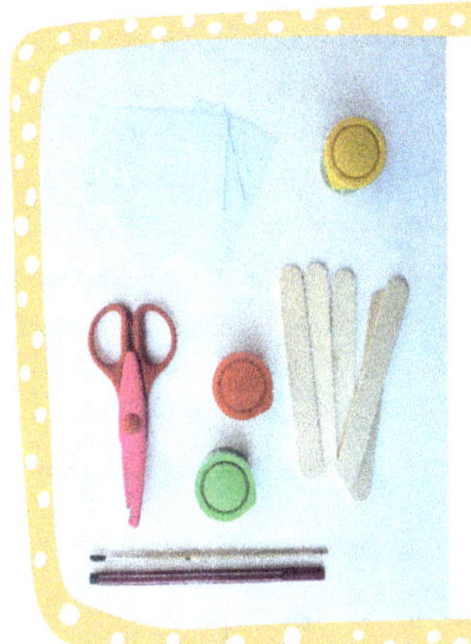

This is what we'll need:

- Popsicle sticks.
- Paint (3 different colors like red, green, and yellow).
- Paint brush.
- Cardboard.
- Markers.
- Scissors.

Teaching our kids math can be quite challenging for parents. A good idea to make it more fun is to mix math with colorful games, like this one we have right here. We can help our 7-8 year olds to recognize hundreds, tens and ones by using different colored popsicle sticks. But don't eat too many popsicles or your belly will hurt!

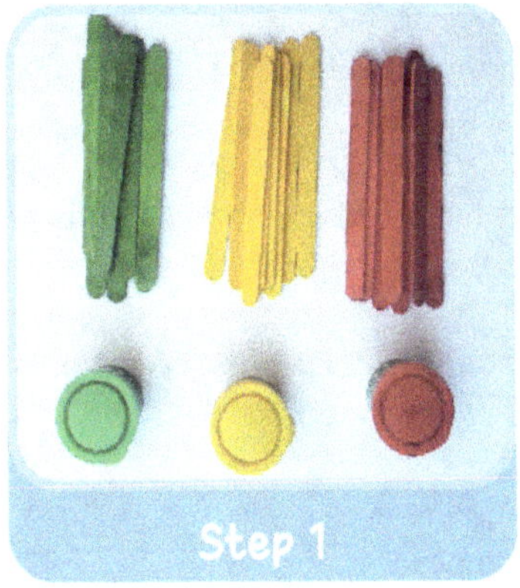

Step 1

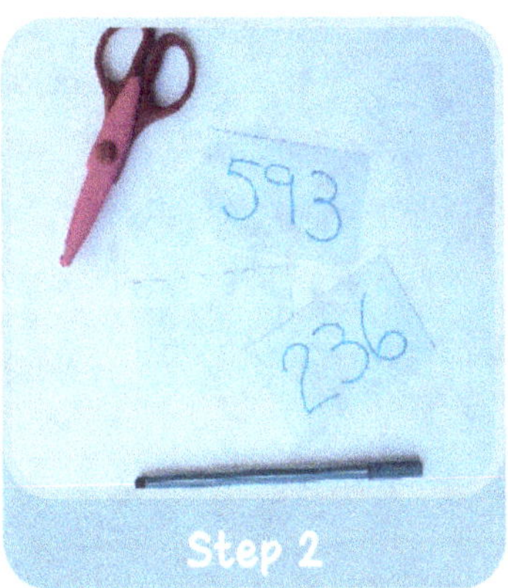

Step 2

Step 1. We need to paint 9 popsicle sticks with the red paint, 9 with green, and 9 with yellow.

Step 2. While the sticks dry, cut small cardboard rectangles where we will write 2 and 3-digit numbers with markers.

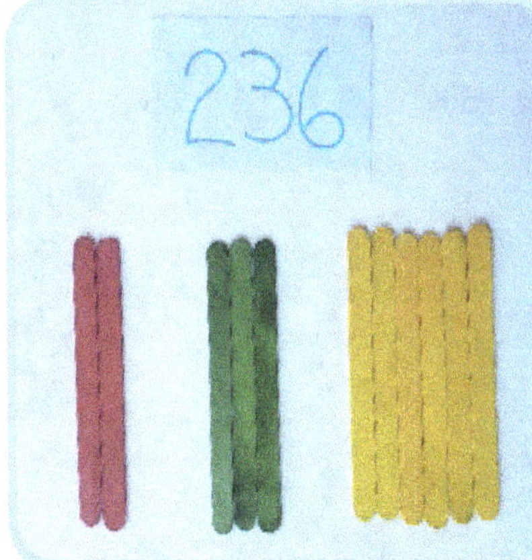

How to play:
- Choose a number.
- The red sticks represent the hundreds, the green ones the tens and the yellow ones the ones.
- Group as many red sticks as there are hundreds in the number we have chosen, then as many green sticks as there are tens and also as many yellow sticks as ones.

For example, if we choose 236, we have 2 red sticks, 3 green sticks and 6 yellow sticks.

Tip: We can use two colors for 1 and 2-digit numbers for younger kids or more than 3 colors for 4+ digits.

MR. GRASS

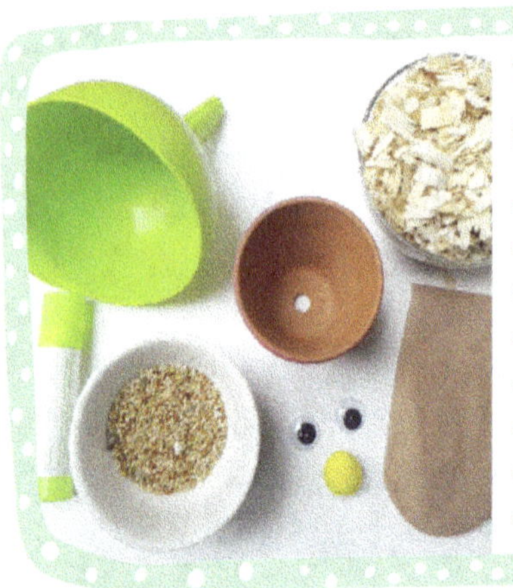

This is what we'll need:

- Flowerpot.
- Funnel.
- Old tights/stockings.
- Sawdust.
- Birdseed.
- Glue.
- Pompom.
- Googly eyes.

Taking care of plants is a great way to teach our kids responsibility, and watching them grow from scratch also helps them learn about the life cycle of a plant. But learning aside, being able to cut their 'hair' and make them different 'hairstyles' sounds fun right?

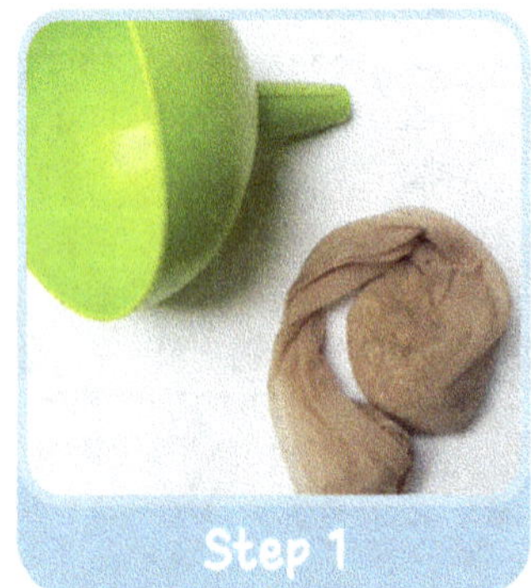

Step 1

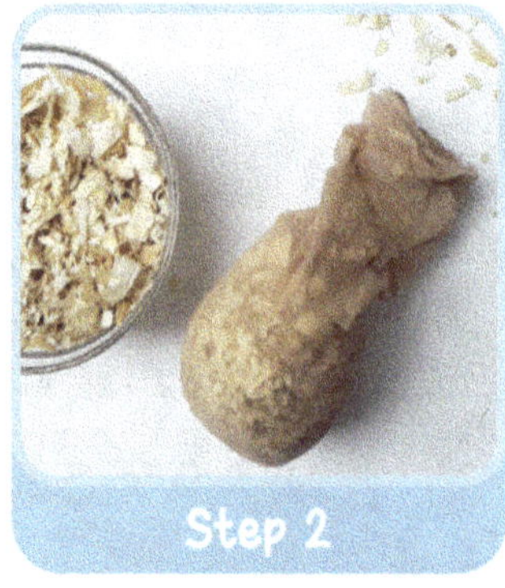

Step 2

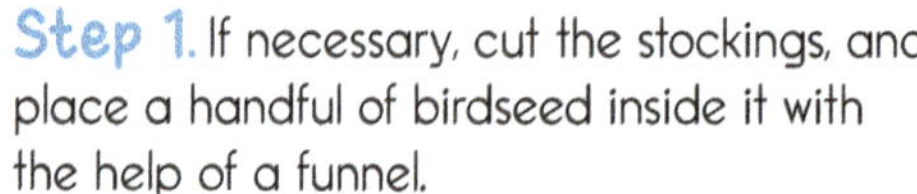

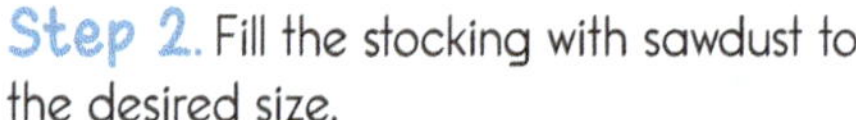

Step 1. If necessary, cut the stockings, and place a handful of birdseed inside it with the help of a funnel.

Step 2. Fill the stocking with sawdust to the desired size.

Step 3. Knot the stocking and give it a more or less round shape.

Step 4. Glue the eyes in place and the pompom as a nose.

Step 5. Put Mr. Grass in his pot and water him every day to see his 'hair' grow!

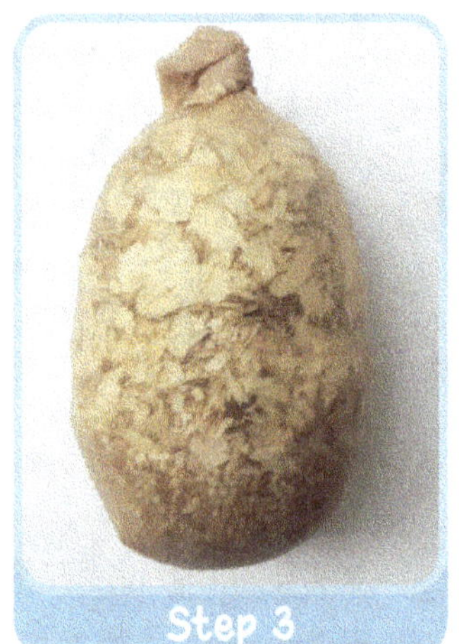

Step 3

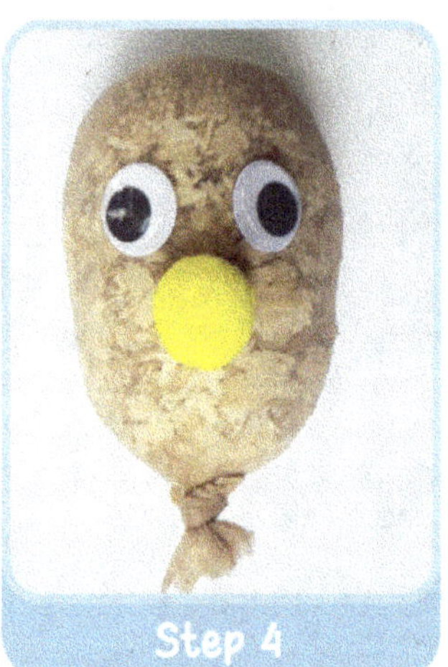

Step 4

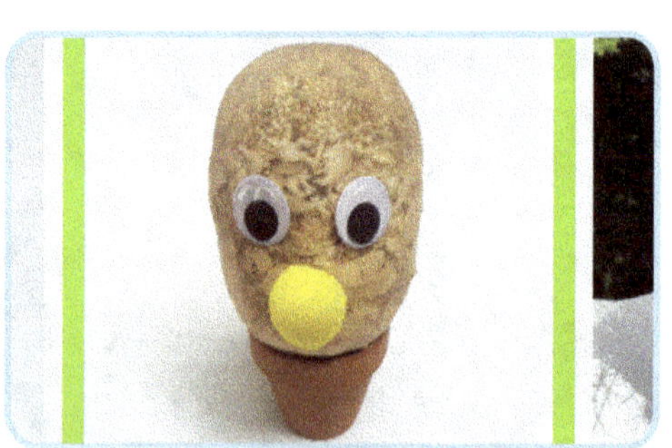

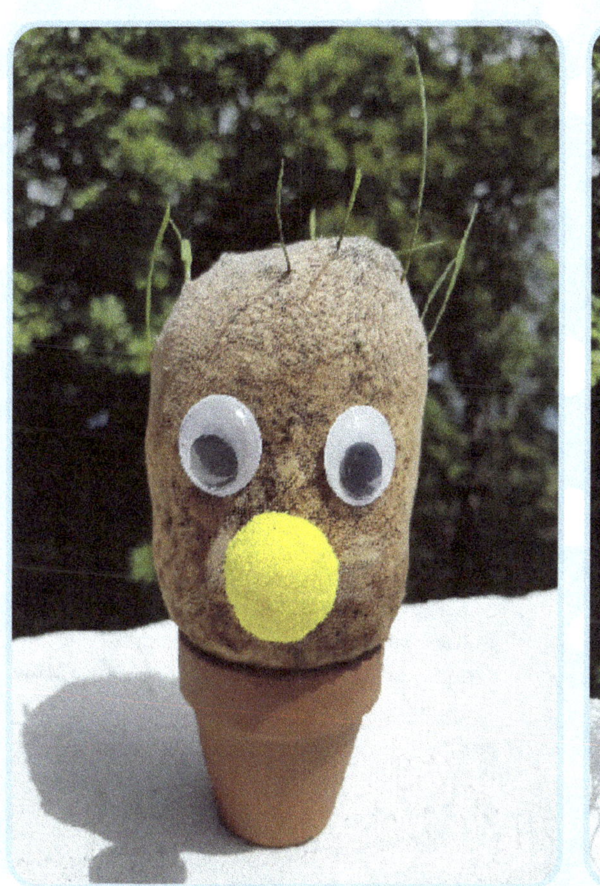 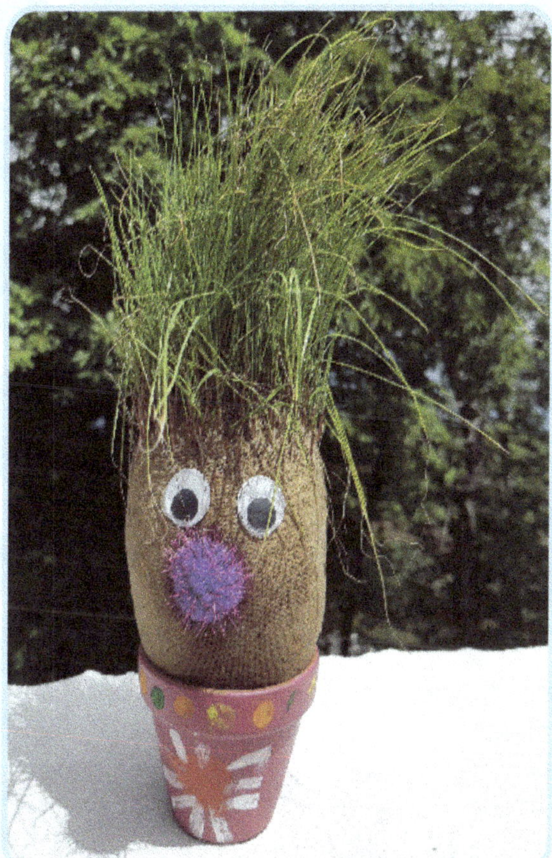

Tip: If we let the 'hair' grow long enough, we can make him different hairstyles and even cut it.

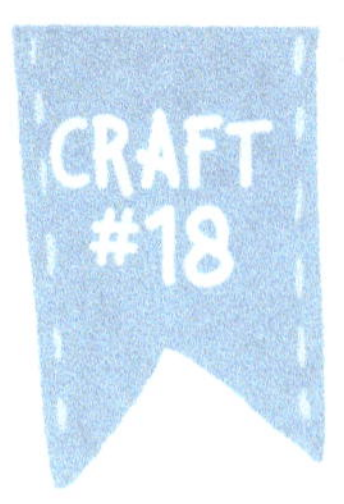

GREATER THAN, LESS THAN, EQUAL TO

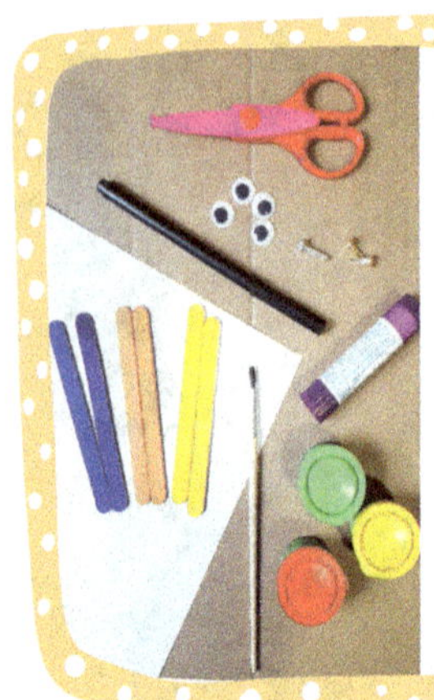

This is what we'll need:

- Popsicle sticks.
- Split pins.
- White paper.
- Black marker.
- Glue or tape.
- Scissors.
- Paint.
- Brush.
- Screw.
- Optional: googly eyes.

Learning to compare numbers can get a bit boring? Our crocodiles can help make learning the terms greater than, less than and equal to a little more fun, do you want to find out?

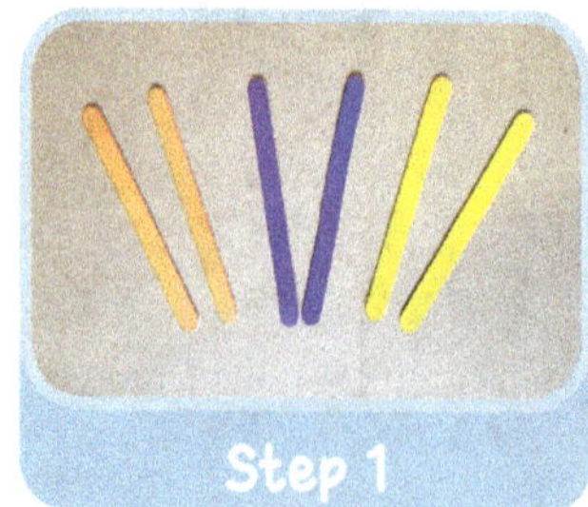

Step 1

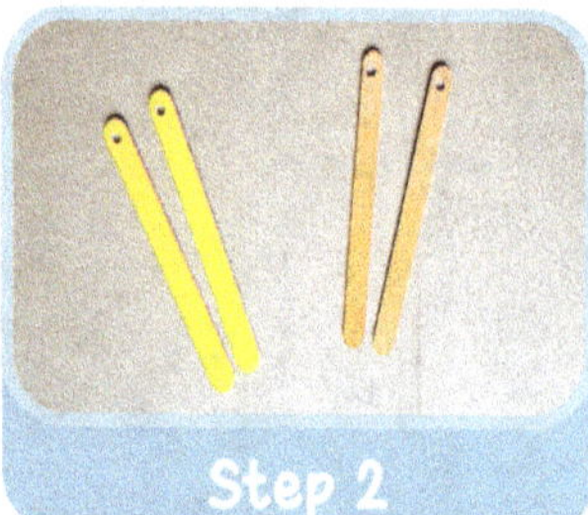

Step 2

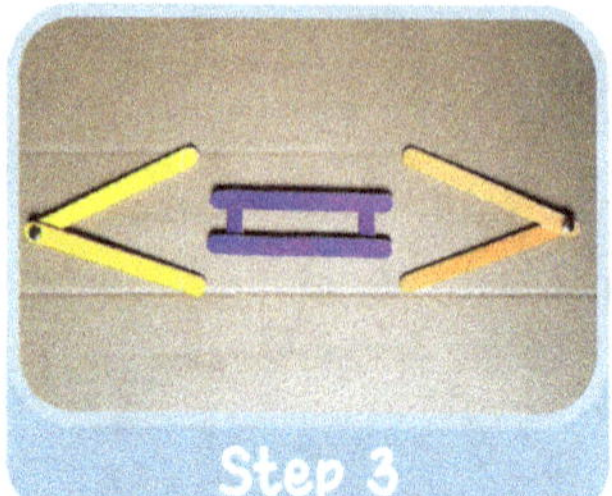

Step 3

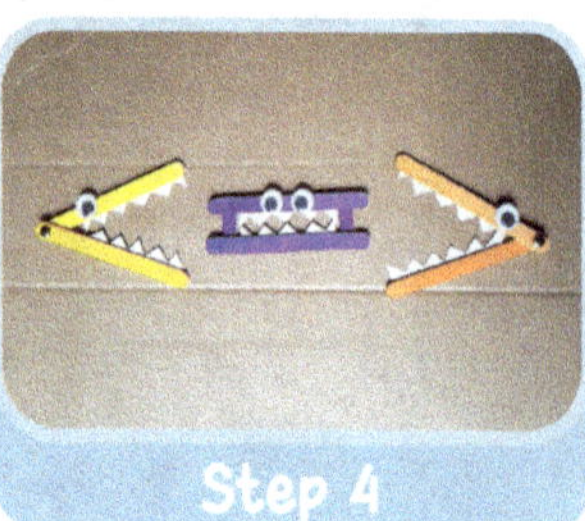

Step 4

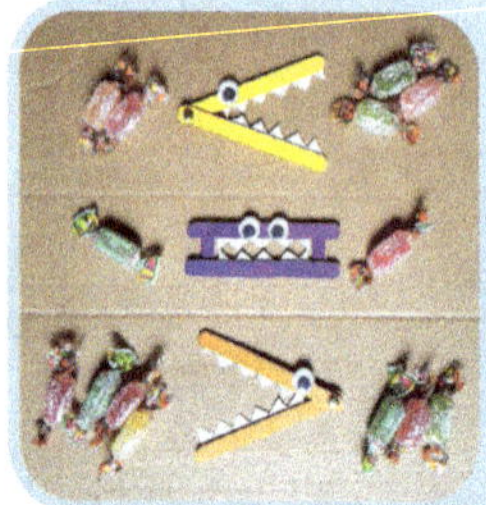

How to play: Make two piles with the same or different amounts of things like pencils, candies, pompoms, etc. and let the kids decide which is the correct symbol to place between them.

Step 1. The first thing we should do is paint the popsicle sticks with our 3 favorite colors. We need to paint 6 sticks, two of each color. If we use popsicle sticks that are already painted, we can jump to the next step.

Step 2. Make a small hole in one of the ends of 4 of the popsicle sticks (there should be two of the same color without any holes). We used a screw, but we can use anything we have on hand. Make sure the hole is big enough to fit the split pin.

Step 3. Put the split pin through the holes of two sticks of the same color to make one of the greater or less than symbols. Repeat with the other two sticks with holes. To join the two sticks without holes, cut two pieces of the same size from another stick (no painting required) and glue them to the back of the colored sticks, so that they are parallel.

Step 4. Cut out sharp teeth and eyes from white paper, draw the details with a black marker and glue/tape them to the back of the popsicle sticks. We can also use googly eyes instead of paper eyes and glue them to the front side.

KERPLUNK

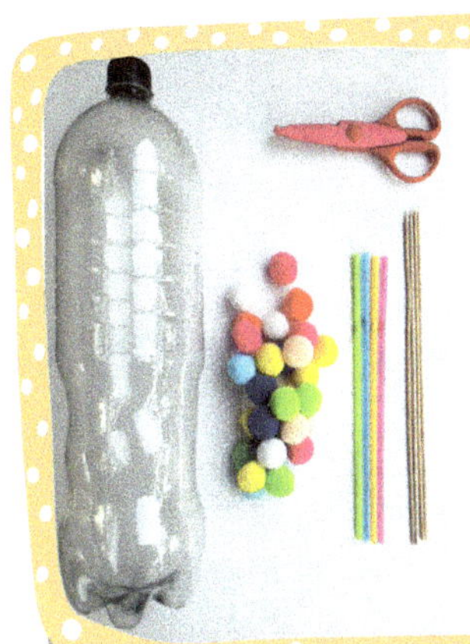

This is what we'll need:

- Plastic bottle.
- Scissors.
- Straws or skewers.
- Pompoms.

KerPlunk is a game that has been around since the 1960s and now we can make our own version. Using a plastic bottle, some straws and pompoms we can improve our kids hand-eye coordination and problem-solving skills, while counting and recognizing colors. How about a little friendly competition?

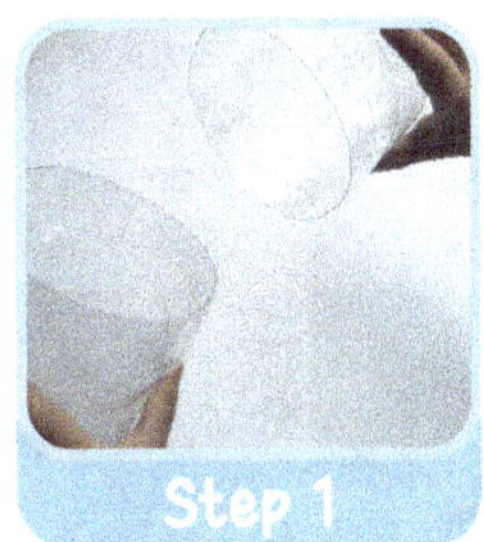
Step 1

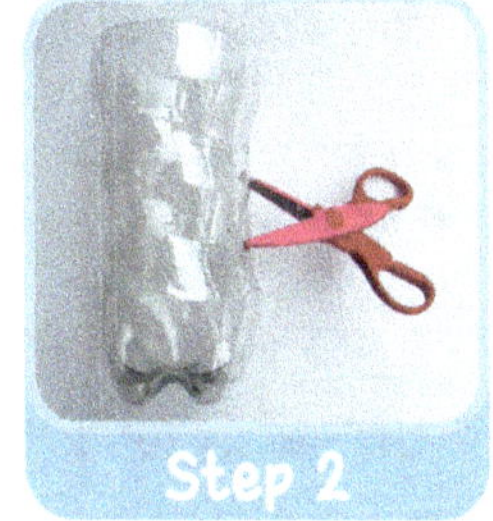
Step 2

Step 1. We cut the upper part of the empty plastic bottle, so that we have an opening at the top and the bottom part is closed.

Step 2. With the scissors, we poke holes large enough to fit the straws around the top half of the bottle. Leave a little space at the top without holes, this is where the pompoms will be placed.

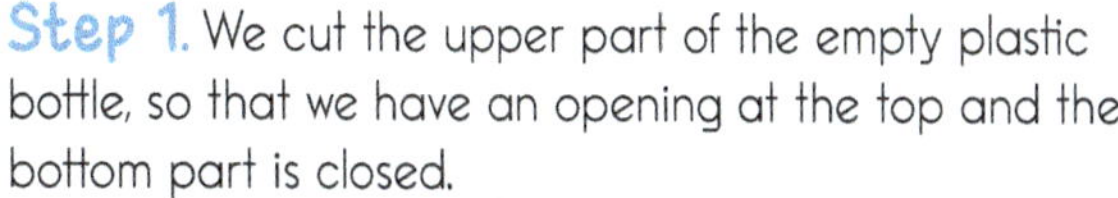

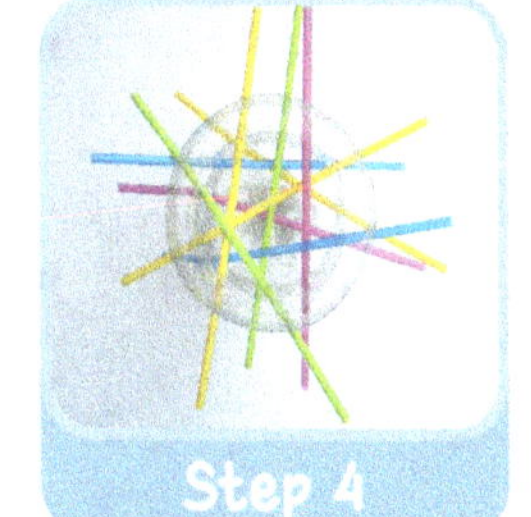
Step 3

Step 4

Step 3. Insert the straws through the holes. We have to place them so that they go from one side of the bottle to the other in all possible directions, forming a grid that prevents the pompoms from falling.

Step 4. Place the pompoms on top of the straws, and make sure they don't fall between them. If there are any slits through which they fall, you can reposition the straws.

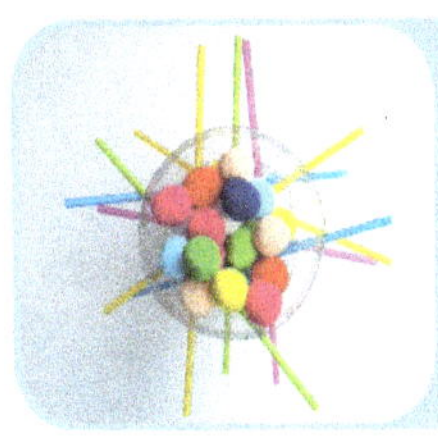

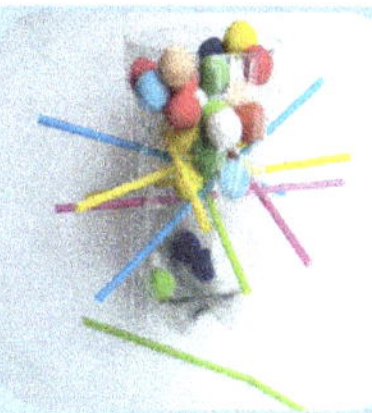

How to play:

- Each player must remove a straw on their turn, trying to drop as few pompoms as possible.
- Once we touch a straw, we have to take that one out.
- The player who drops fewer pompoms wins.

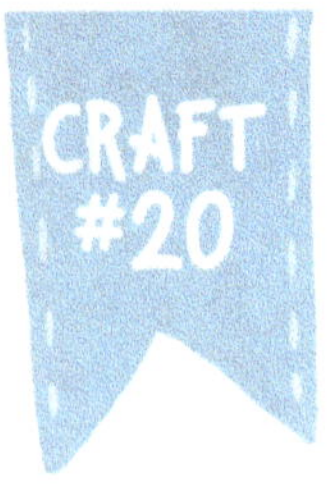

CARTON BOAT

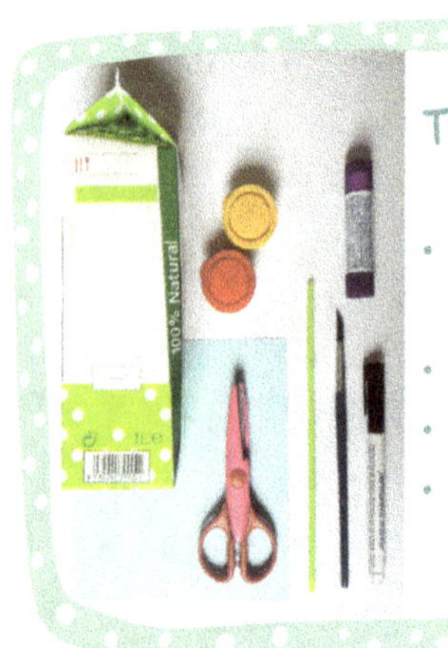

Most crafts aren't made to survive a bubble bath, but what if I told you that we have something in mind that our kids can take into the bathtub, the beach or the pool? Pour yourself a glass of juice and please don't throw away the carton!

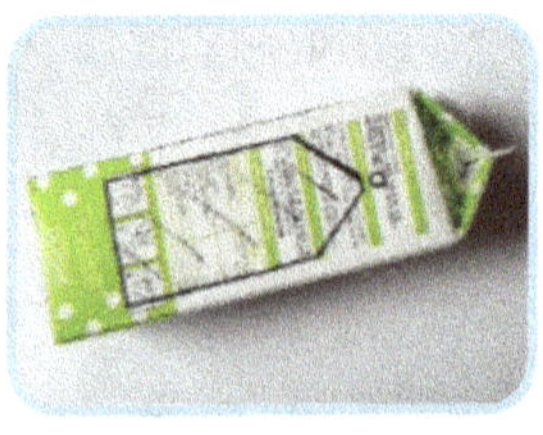
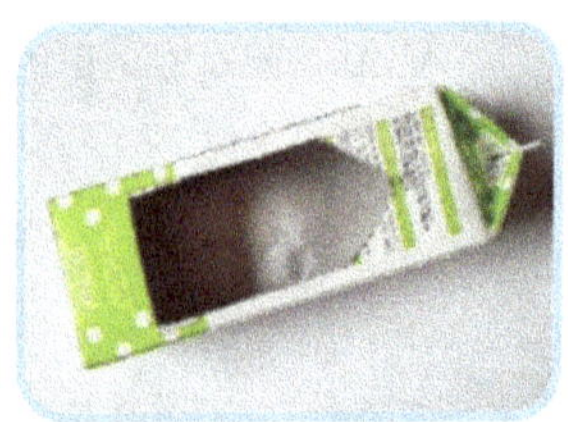

Step 1. After washing and drying the milk or juice carton, we use the marker to design our boat on it. With the carton placed sideways, we start by drawing an opening in the side that's now facing up, leaving space in the front to place the sail later. Then we can add details such as stripes, portholes or an anchor.

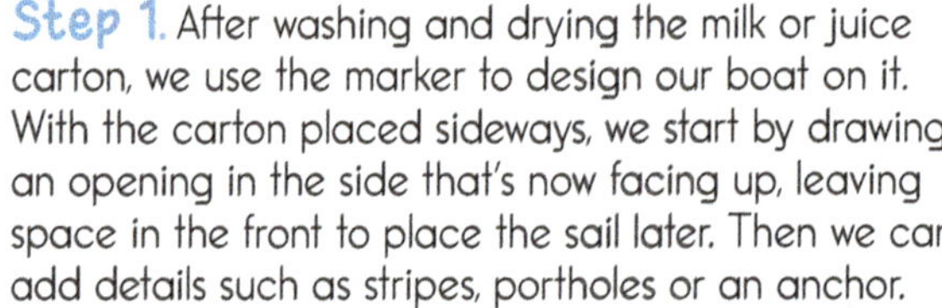

Step 2. Use the scissors to cut the opening on the upper side and a small hole a little towards the front of the boat. We will use that hole later to place the straw that will serve as a mast for our sail.

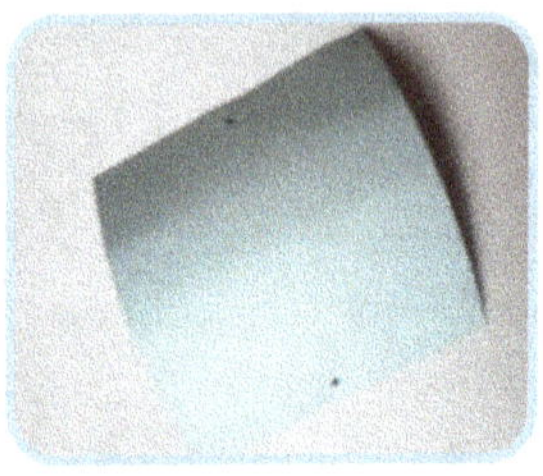
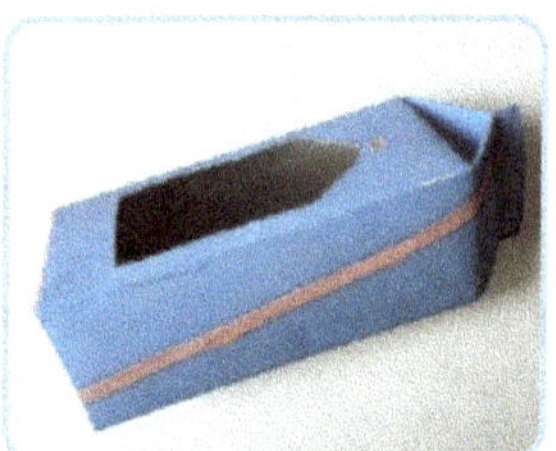

Step 3. Cut a 20x20 cm or 8"x8" cardboard square and give it a rounded shape using our hands. This is going to be our sail, so we need to make two small holes to fit it into the straw. The holes will go right in the center of two opposite sides, 1 cm from the edge.

Step 4. Paint the boat and sail. You can make it as colorful and fun as you want, but remember to use waterproof paint!

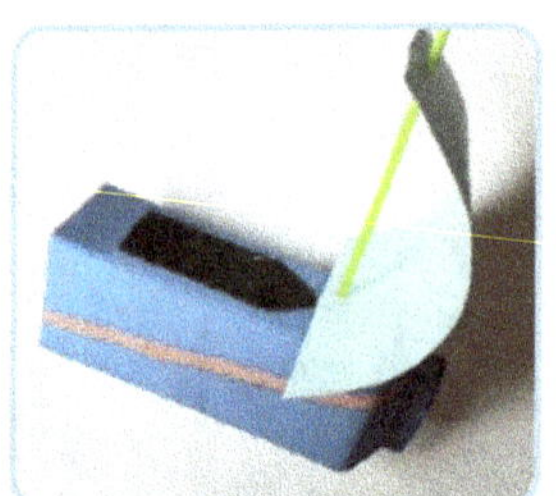
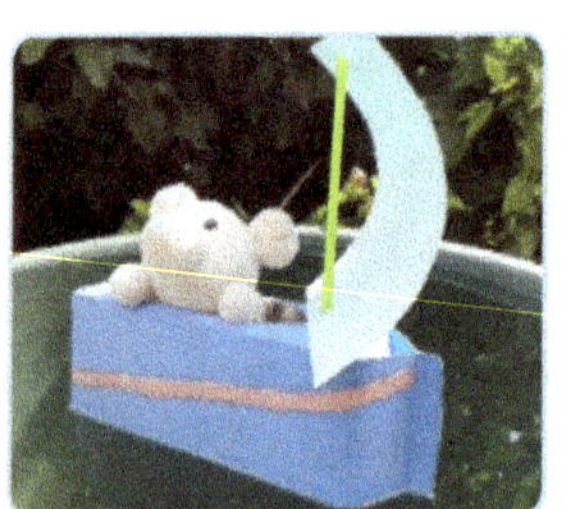

Step 5. Next, we insert the straw into the hole we made earlier and secure it with a little glue. Finally, we put the sail in place by inserting the straw through the two holes. We can also secure it with a little glue.

Step 6. Sail away!

PAPER SPINNER

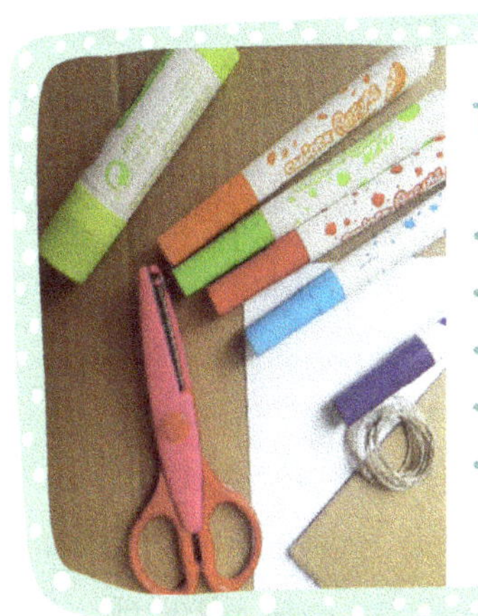

This is what we'll need:

- Cardboard and paper.
- Markers.
- Scissors.
- Glue.
- Twine.

Here's a super simple, super fun craft to keep our kids entertained: a paper spinner.

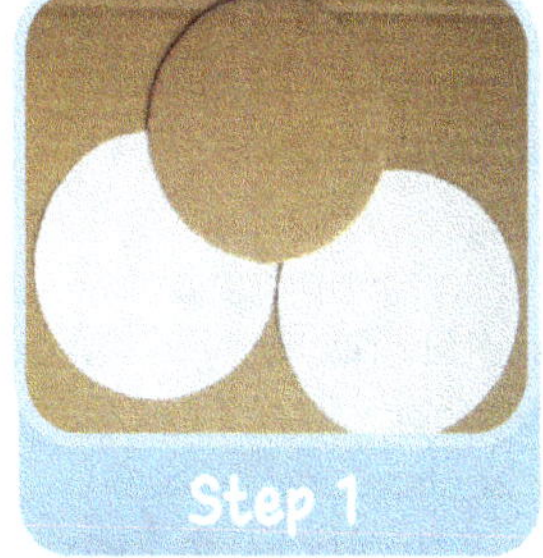

Step 1

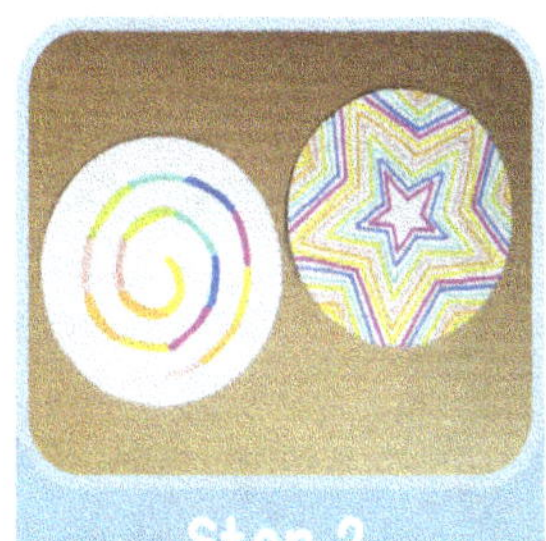

Step 2

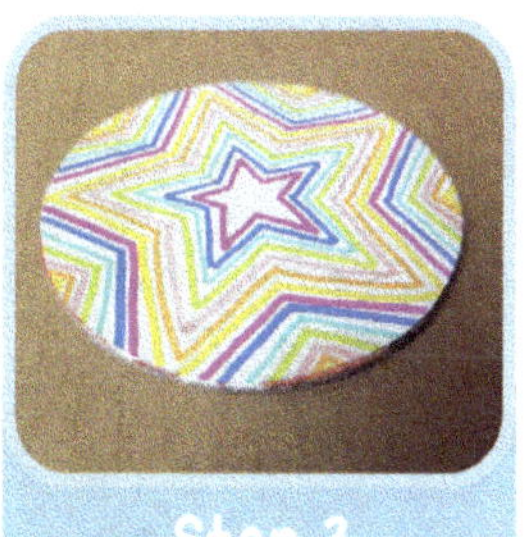

Step 3

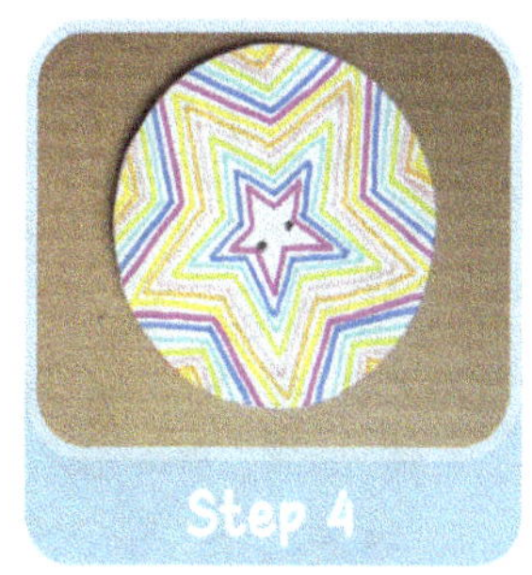

Step 4

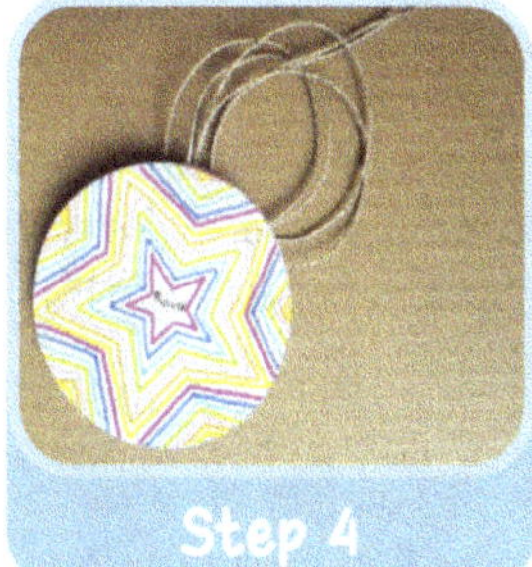

Step 4

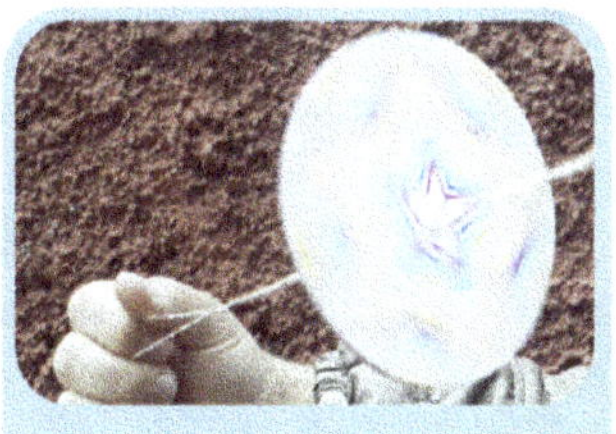

How to play:
Take one end of the rope in each hand, with the cardboard circle roughly in the middle, and twist it as much as you can. Now pull and relax the twine to see the circle spin.

Step 1. Cut out a cardboard circle and two white paper circles of the same size.

Step 2. Draw a colorful spiral (or any other fun design you can think of) in the two white circles using the markers, the more colorful the better!

Step 3. Glue each drawing to one side of the cardboard circle.

Step 4. Poke two holes in the center of the circle.

Step 5. Thread a 25-30 inch twine through the two holes and knot them.

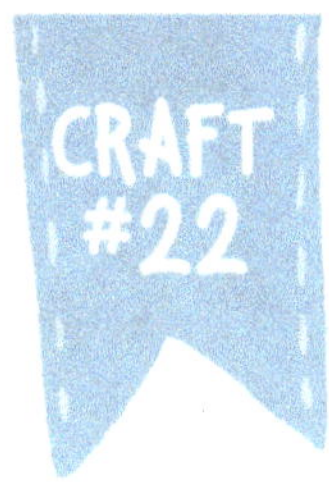

BOOKMARKS

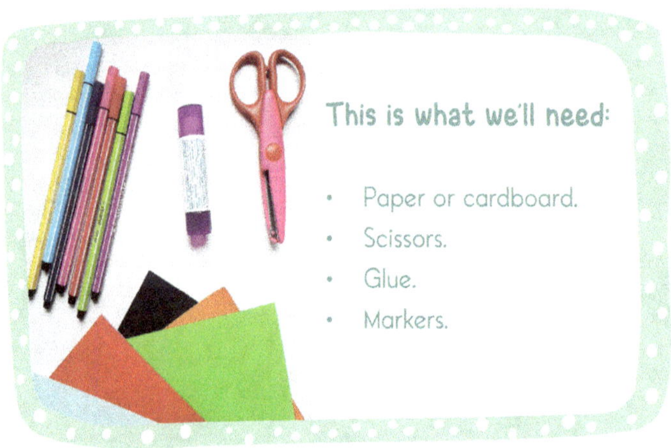

Reading is fundamental in our kids' development, since they not only learn new sounds and vocabulary, but it also awakens their imagination, helps them develop their concentration, and reinforces their communication skills. With today's craft we will create little friends that will help them remember which page they stayed on and make reading even more fun.

Step 1. We must start by cutting 4"x4" or 12x12 cm square pieces of paper or cardboard in our favorite color.

Step 2. Fold the square piece of paper or cardboard horizontally in half and unfold it. Next, fold it in half again in the opposite direction and unfold it. We should end up with a cross-shaped crease that divides our piece of paper into four smaller squares.

Step 3. Cut out one of the small squares. That leaves us with a V-shaped piece of paper made up of three small squares.

Step 4. In the side squares, draw a diagonal line connecting its upper and lower vertices, so that it is divided into two triangles.

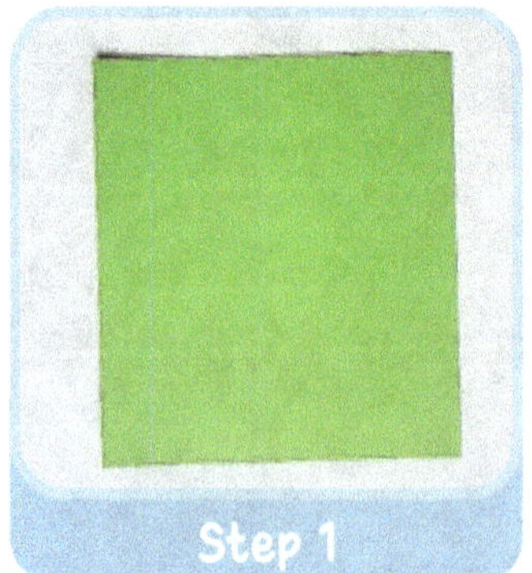

Step 1

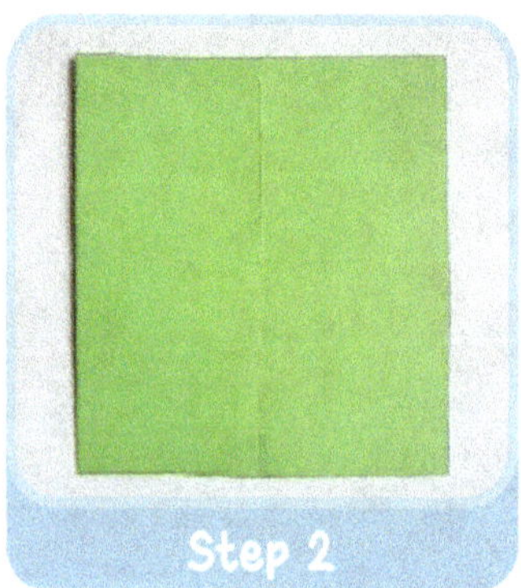

Step 2

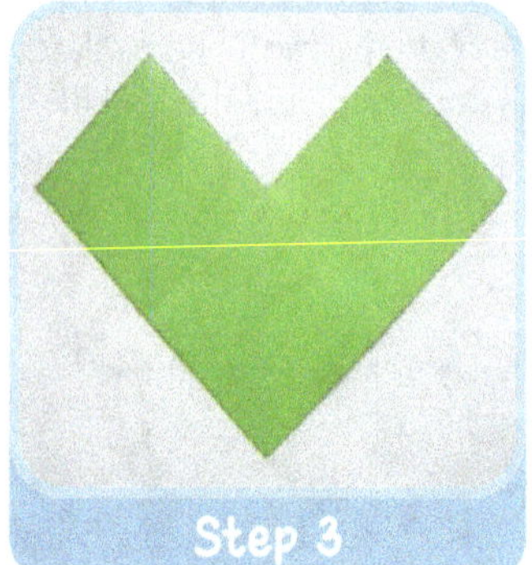

Step 3

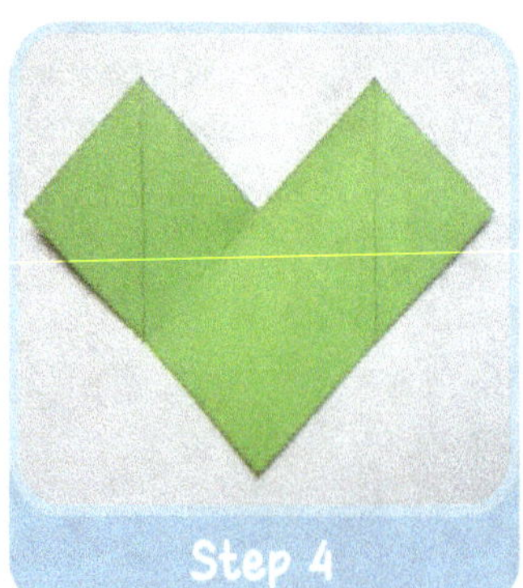

Step 4

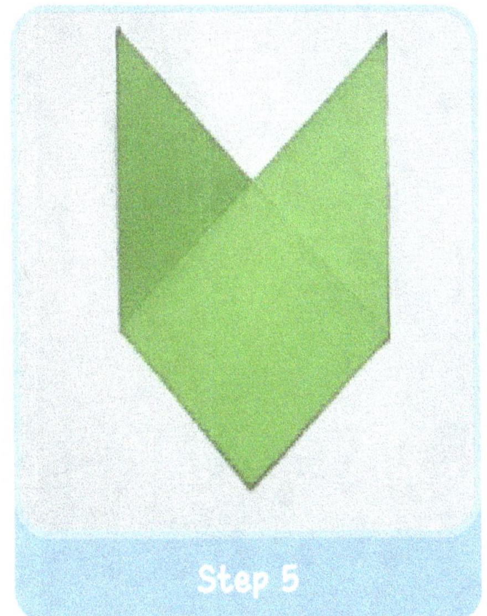

Step 5

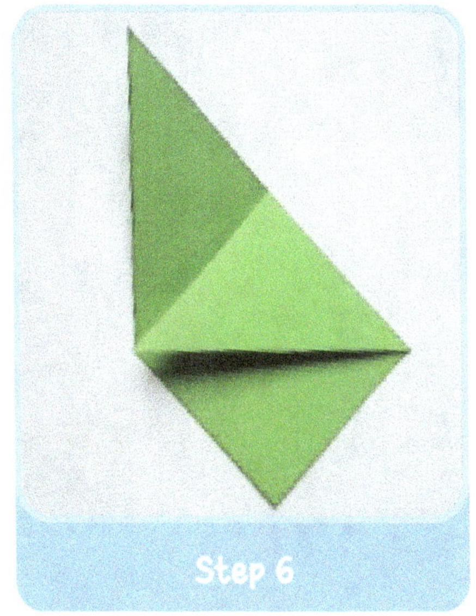

Step 6

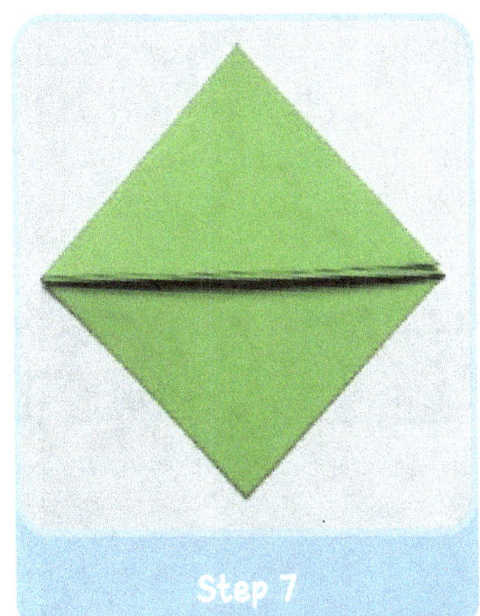

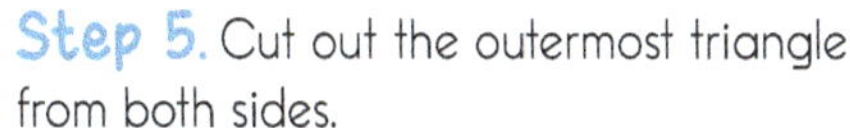

Step 7

Step 5. Cut out the outermost triangle from both sides.

Step 6. Now, fold one of the triangles inward, so that it sits on top of the central square.

Step 7. Next, fold the other one inward too, but this time we have to glue it to the first triangle. This way they make some sort of pocket where the pages of the books will fit.

Step 8. Now that the basic structure is ready, we can let our imagination fly and decorate the bookmarks with markers and pieces of paper or cardboard as we like best. We can make fruits, animals, characters...

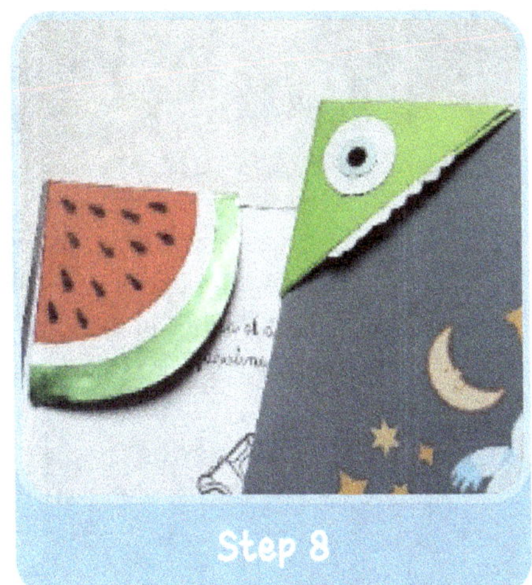

Step 8

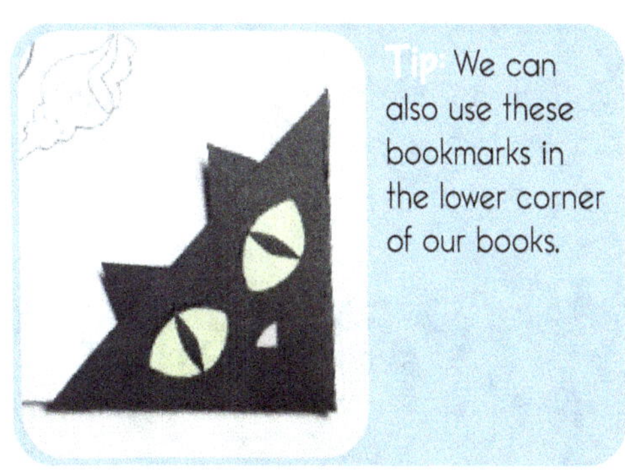

Tip: We can also use these bookmarks in the lower corner of our books.

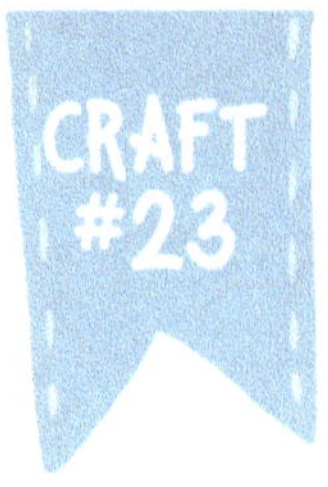

WATER WALKING

This is what we'll need:

- 7 glasses.
- Food coloring or ink (red, yellow, and blue).
- Water.
- Paper towels.

Here we have a science experiment that is ideal to explain the ability of water to 'walk' on paper and also the colors that appear when mixing primary colors. It takes almost no time, we need just a few materials and the result is a beautiful rainbow!

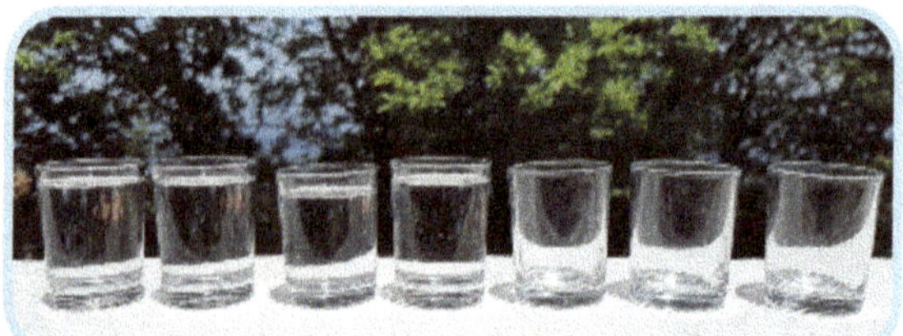

Step 1. Fill four glasses with water and leave the other three empty.

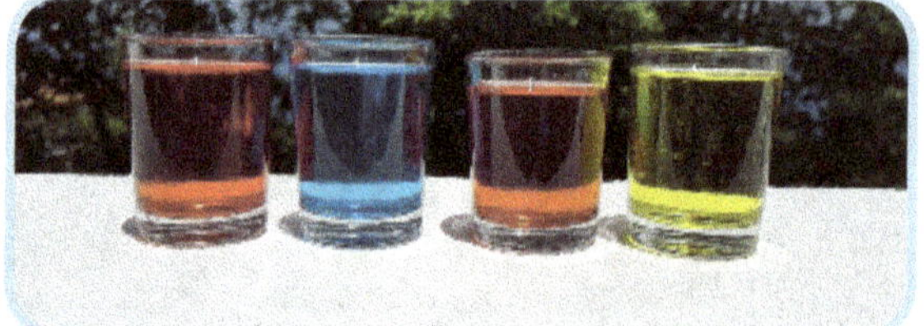

Step 2. Put red food coloring in two of the full glasses, blue in another one and yellow in the other one left.

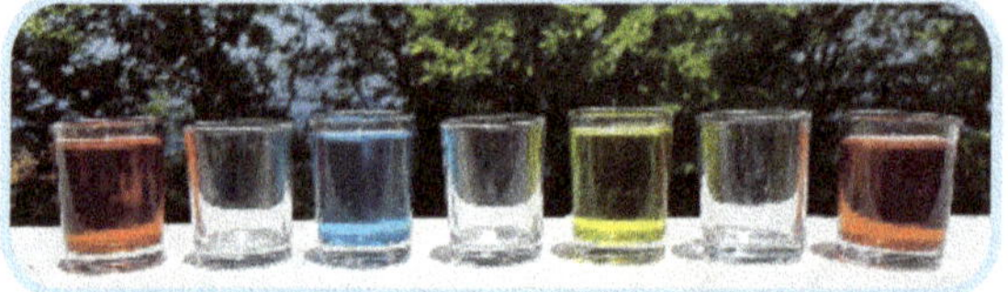

Step 3. Arrange the seven glasses in a row, in this order: red-empty-blue-empty-yellow-empty-red.

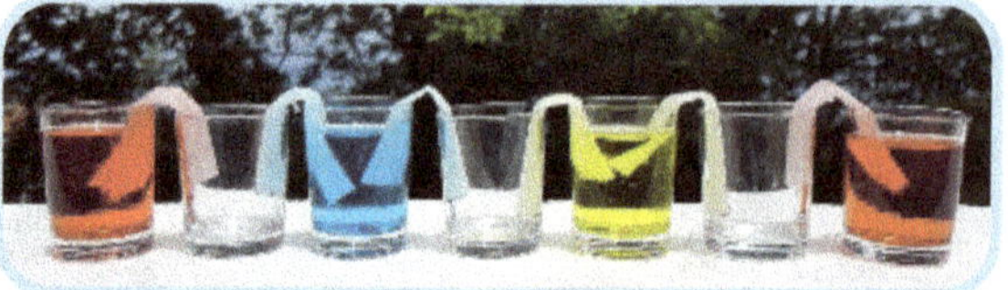

Step 4. Take a paper towel, cut it in half, roll it into a thin rectangle, and then fold it in half. Put one half in a glass and the other in the glass next to it. Repeat until all the glasses are connected.

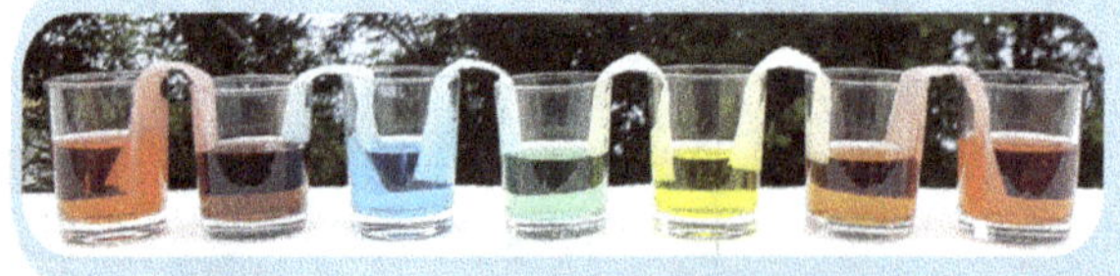

Tip. Cut all the paper towels before putting them in the glasses, so all the colors start to 'walk' at the same time. In just a few seconds we've made a rainbow! Pretty cool, right?

FAIRY JAR

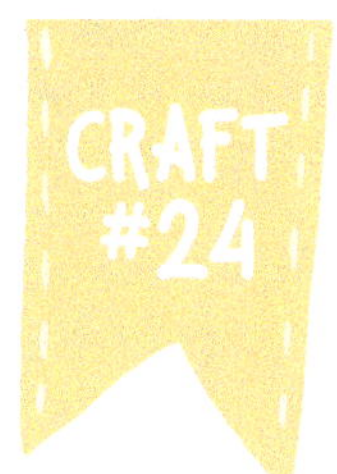

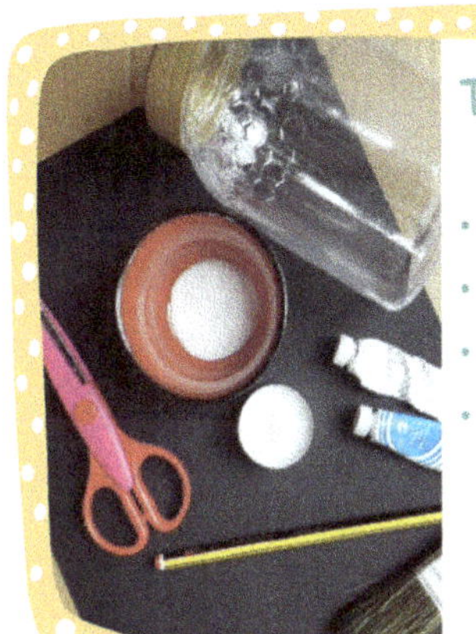

This is what we'll need:

- Empty jar.
- Paint.
- White glue.
- Paintbrush.

- Black paper.
- Pencil.
- Scissors.
- Tealight.

Looking for a DIY night light for your kid's room? Then you don't have to search anymore! Today we are going to decorate a jar that can be a fantastic night light and a very cute decoration that our little ones will love.

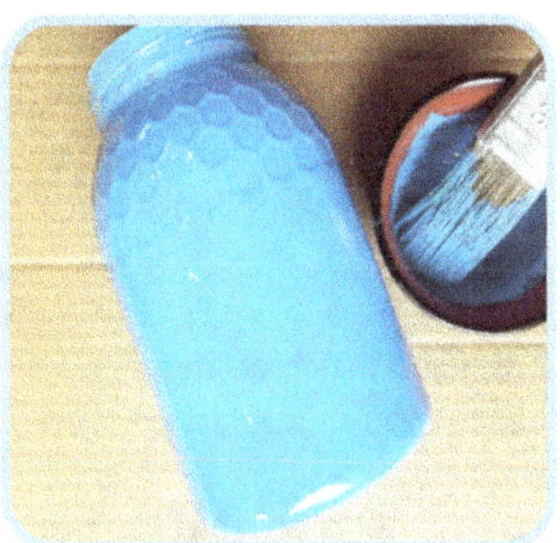

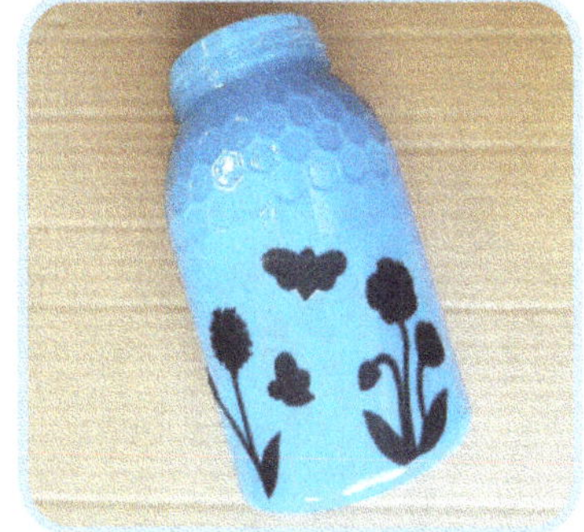

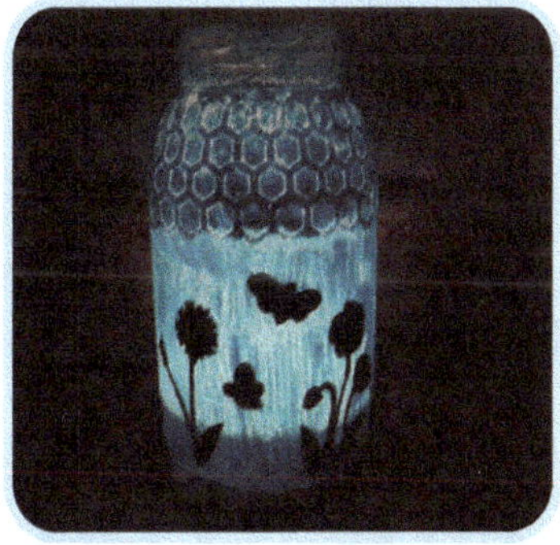

Step 1. Instead of buying special glass/plastic paint for our jars, mix normal paint and white glue in equal parts. Apply a thin layer of this mix to the inside of the jar so that it's completely covered but the light from the tealight can be seen through it.

Step 2. Decorate the jar with black silhouettes. For this we have several options: print them ready to glue, draw and cut them on black paper, or draw them directly on the outside of the jar with permanent markers or paint. We made some drawings with a pencil on black paper, cut them out and glued them to the outside of the jar also with white glue.

Step 3. Place a tealight inside the jar. Keep in mind that it's better to use LED tealights if our kids are going to handle it, thus preventing them from playing with real fire.

As we used a honey jar, we made flower and bee silhouettes, but there are many options: fairies, butterflies, elves... We can even make them with a Christmas or Halloween theme.

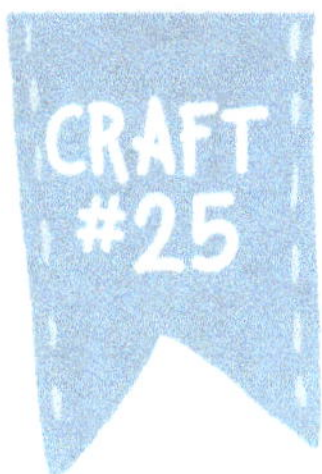

POPSICLE TREE

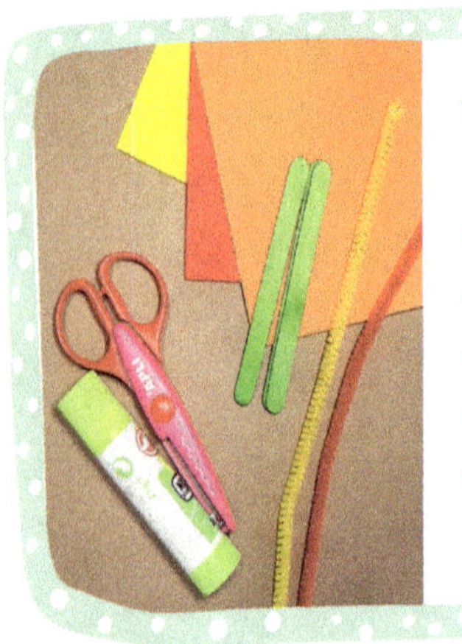

This is what we'll need:

- Popsicle sticks.
- Glue.
- Scissors.
- Cardstock or foam.
- Decoration: small pompoms, bells, pipe cleaners.

Here's a creative and colorful Christmas craft, our kids will have a lot of fun. They can also decorate their room or the family Christmas tree with their cute creations, so let's get to work!

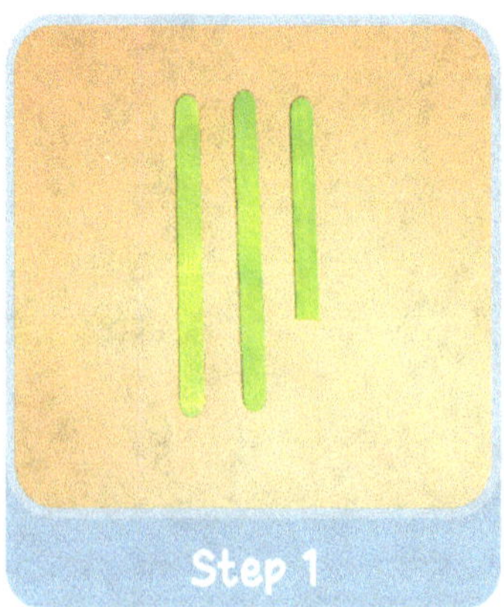

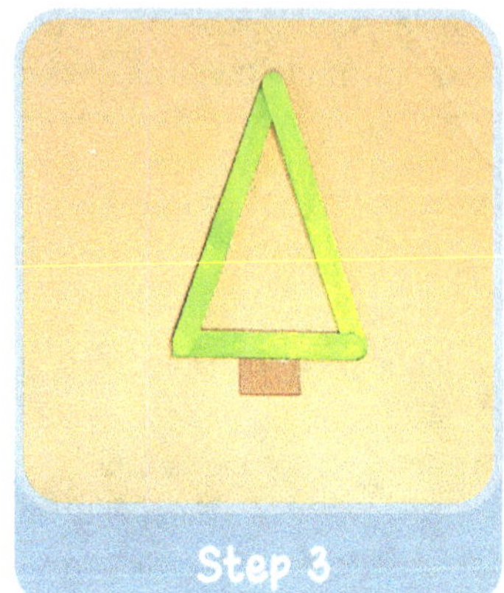

Step 1. We need 3 green popsicle sticks, we can paint them or use some that are already dyed. Cut a piece from one of the sticks to make it shorter than the others.

Step 2. Glue the three sticks together to form a triangle.

Step 3. Cut out a brown cardstock or foam square to make the tree trunk and glue it to the bottom back of the triangle.

Step 4. Cut out a yellow cardstock or foam star and glue it to the top of the triangle.

Step 5. Decorate the tree with little pompoms, bells, pipe cleaners, or whatever we want.

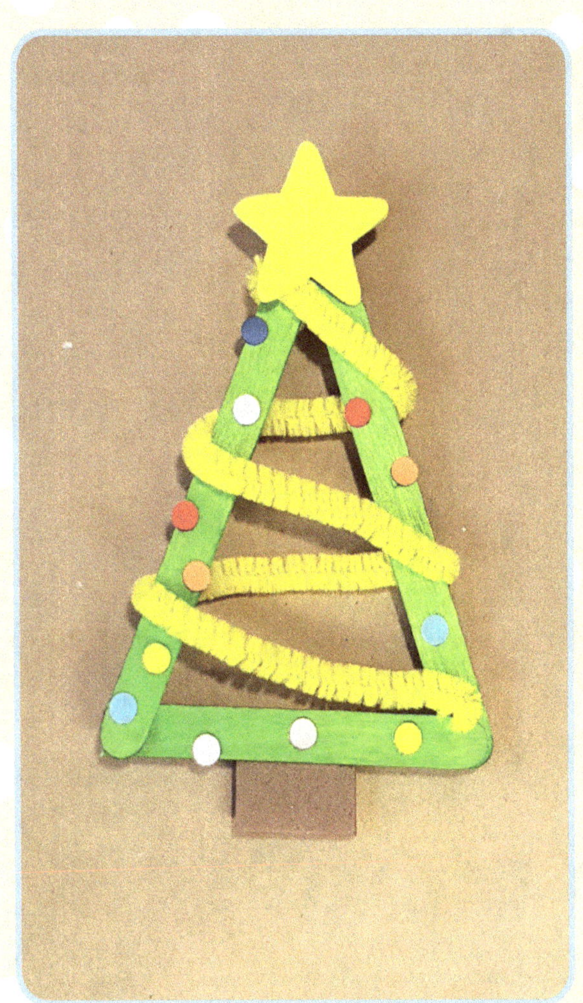

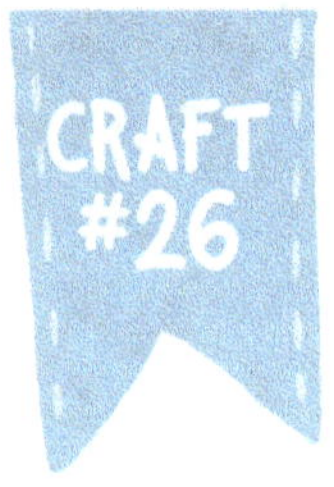

WINDMILL

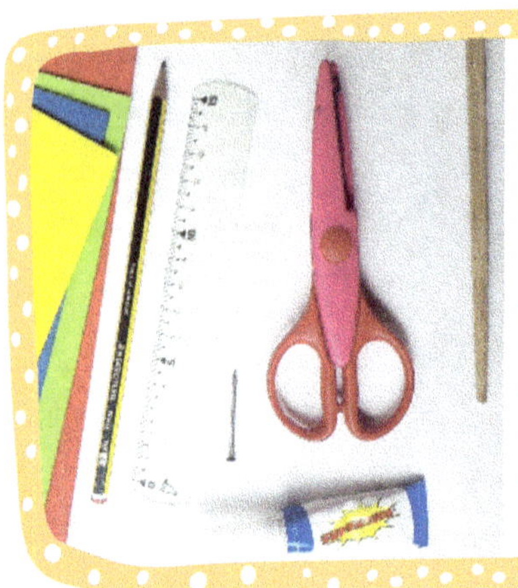

This is what we'll need:

- Paper, foam or cardboard.
- Pencil.
- Ruler.
- Scissors.
- Glue.
- Pin or nail.
- Stick.

Windmills are a great way to teach our kids the force of the wind and explain its different uses, such as grinding grain or producing energy. This is an easy craft, full of color and with which we can decorate our garden or a flower pot.

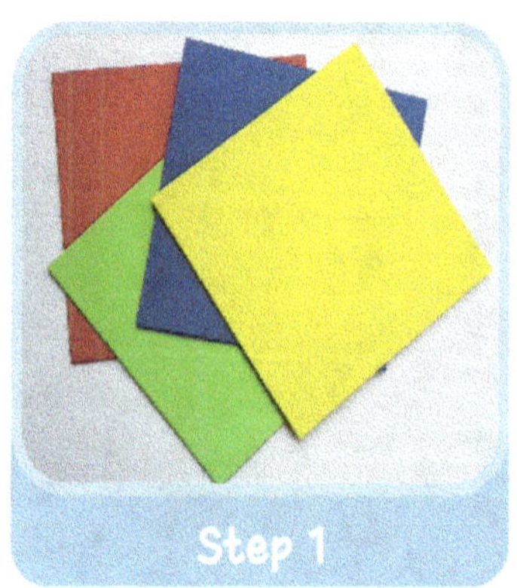

Step 1

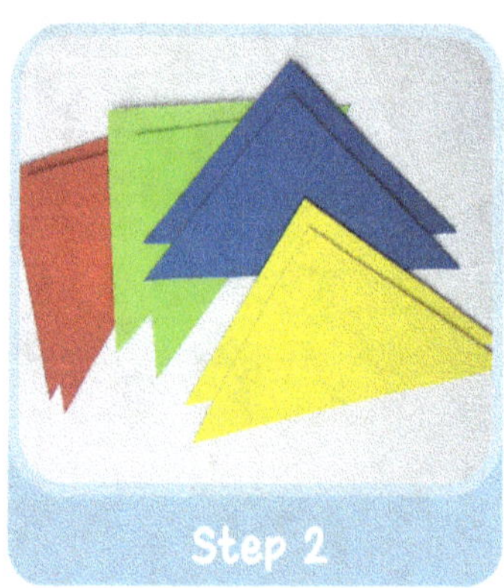

Step 2

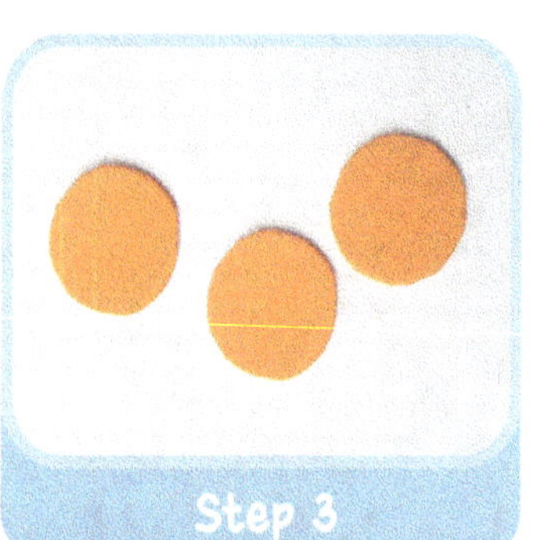

Step 3

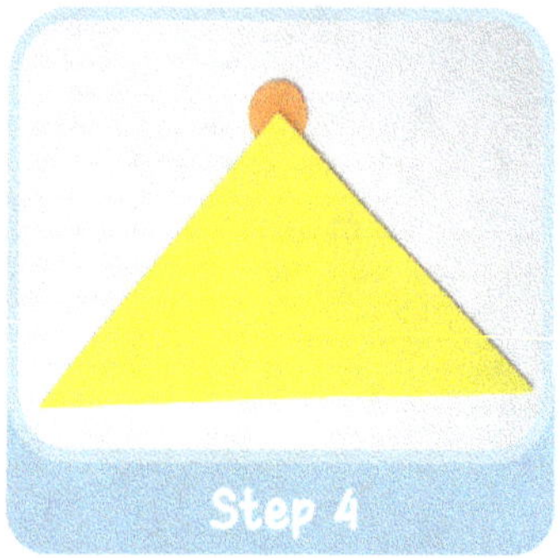

Step 4

Step 1. Cut out 4 squares of paper, foam or cardboard of different colors (although we can make them all the same color, whatever we prefer).

Step 2. Crease and cut each square along one of its diagonals. After this we'll have 8 triangles, two of each color, with a right angle.

Step 3. Cut out three 0.5" diameter circles of the color we like the most.

Step 4. Glue the right angle of one triangle to one of the circles we just cut out.

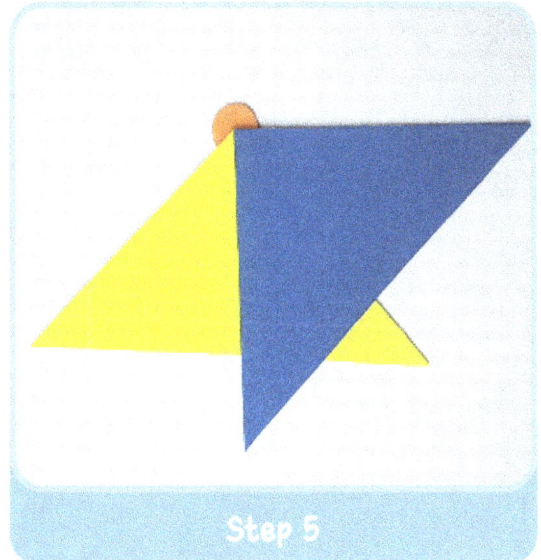

Step 5

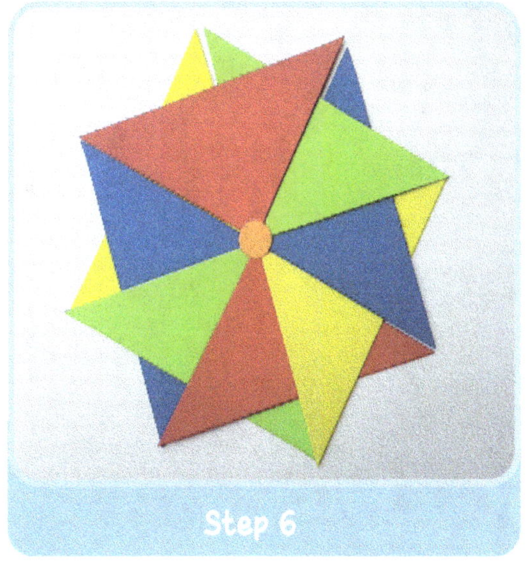

Step 6

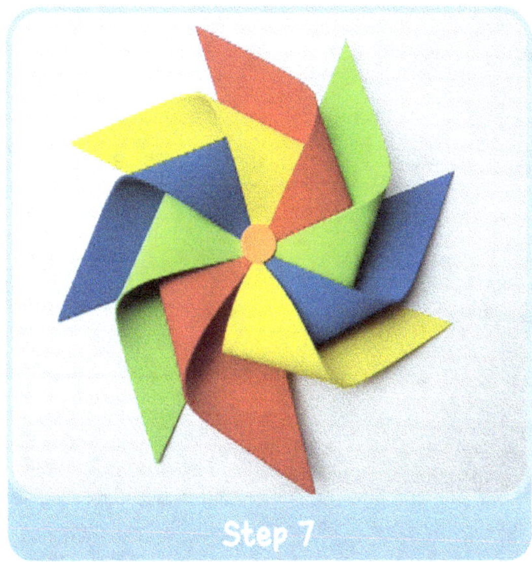

Step 7

Step 5. Glue the next triangle in the same way, but taking care that it is perpendicular to the previous one.

Step 6. Keep gluing the other triangles in this way. After placing them all, glue another circle on top to make it more stable.

Step 7. Fold the free vertex of each triangle inward and glue it to the center of the figure. When we're done, glue the last circle that we had cut out on top of all those vertices to secure them and let all the glue dry.

Step 8. Use a pin or small nail to attach the windmill to a stick. We can paint the nail to make it more beautiful, but this is optional.

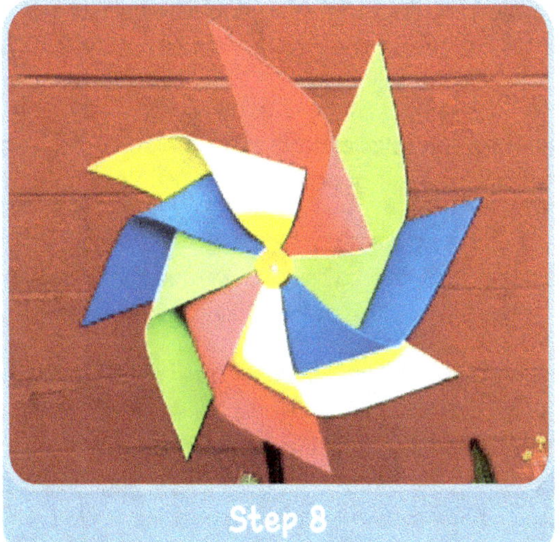

Step 8

Tip: If we use a branch, we must make sure that it doesn't have anything that touches the windmill or it won't spin. Also, we can make a small paper tube to cover the back of the nail.

FISHING CUPS

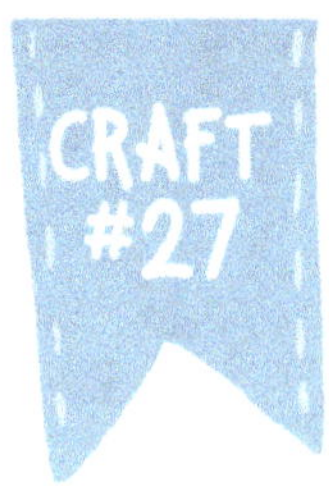

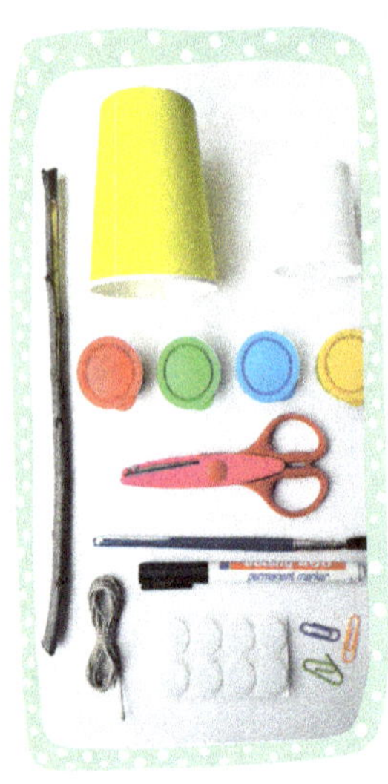

This is what we'll need:

Fish:
- Cups.
- Pipe cleaners, thread or thin wire.
- Optional: googly eyes and cardboard fins.

Fishing rod:
- Stick.
- Thread.
- Paper clip, pipe cleaners or thin wire.

Supplies:
- Paint.
- Paint brush.
- Scissors.
- Black marker.

Would you like to go fishing without leaving home? With this craft our kids will not only have fun creating a whole world of colorful sea creatures, they will also be able to play with them as much as they want! The best part is that we can recycle materials that we have at home and let our imagination fly. Ready?

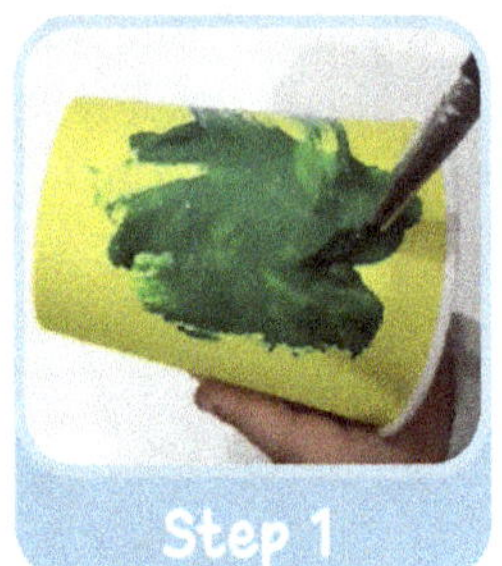

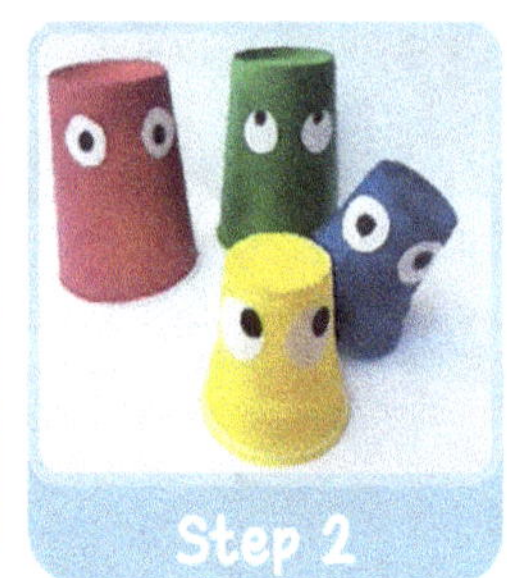

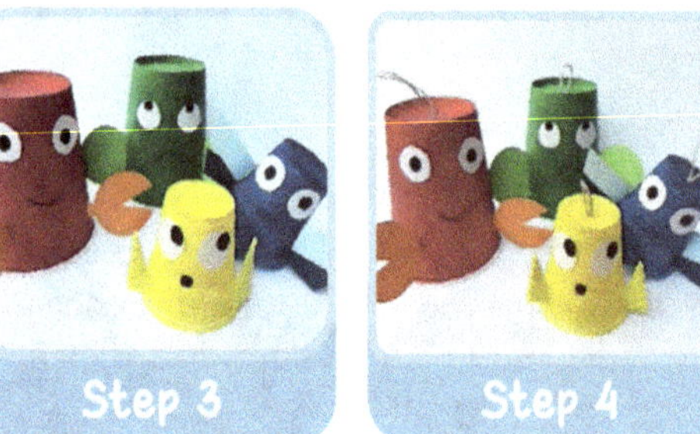

Step 1. We are going to use paper and plastic cups in different sizes, this way there are going to be easier fish to catch than others. We can use as many sizes as you want and also the more fish the better! The first thing we need to do is paint all the cups with our favorite colors, I chose blue, green, red and yellow.

Step 2. For the eyes we have a few options: we can paint circles or use white stickers and draw a black dot with a marker or we can use googly eyes, this is totally up to us!

Step 3. After the paint is dry, we are going to decorate our fish. We can add cardboard fins or claws if we decided to throw a crab or two, but don't forget their smiles!

Step 4. With the fish ready to go for a swim, open a small hole on top of the cup. With a pipe cleaner, some thread or thin wire, make a loop, insert it through the hole and make a knot on the inside part of the cup. We can make the loops bigger or smaller depending on how difficult to catch we want the fish to be.

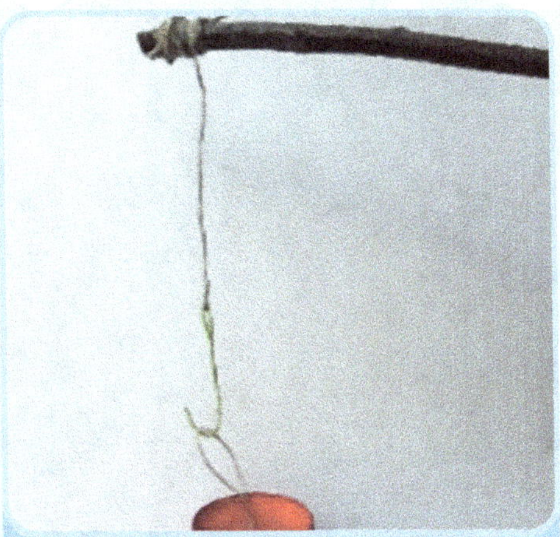

 To make the fishing rod, we need a small stick. First, we tie a piece of thread to one of the ends of the stick, and then we tie a paper clip to the other end of the piece of thread. We can also use pipe cleaners or thin wire in an 's' shape.

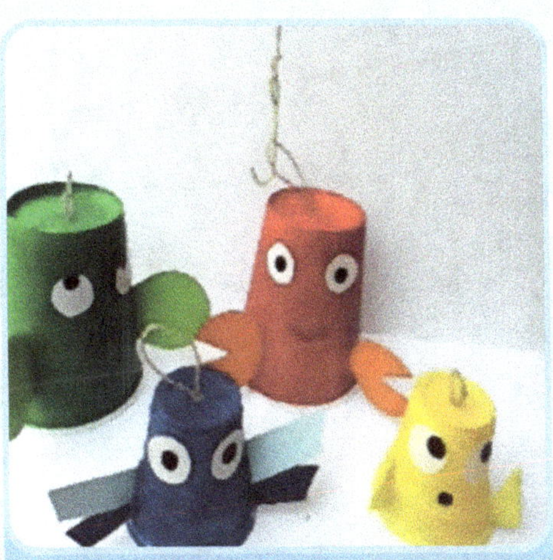

 Grab our under the sea friends and have fun!

Tip: We can use this craft to help fix concepts like first, second, third, last, bigger, smaller, and even draw letters or numbers to our fish.

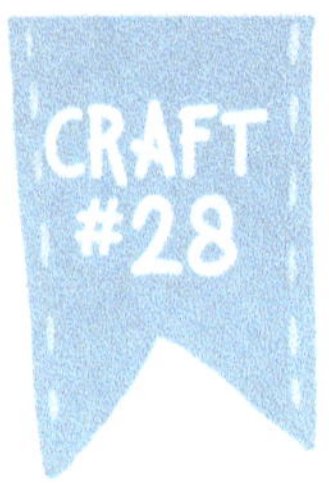

MY PLACE IN THE WORLD

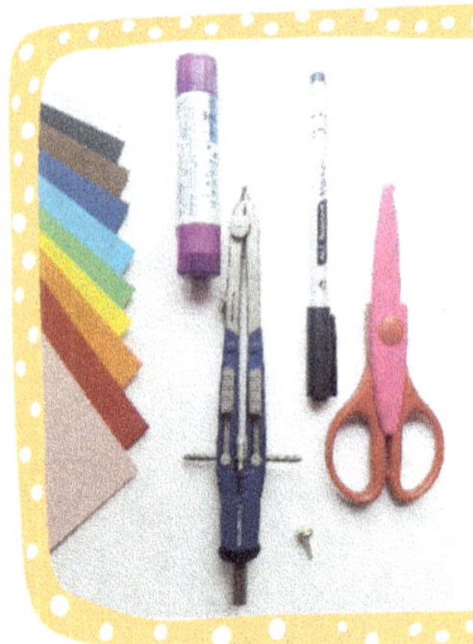

This is what we'll need:

- Foam or cardboard.
- Compass.
- Scissors.
- Glue.
- Markers.
- Ring or split pin.

Most kids are curious about their place in the world around us, that's why today we have this craft called 'my place in the world' here.

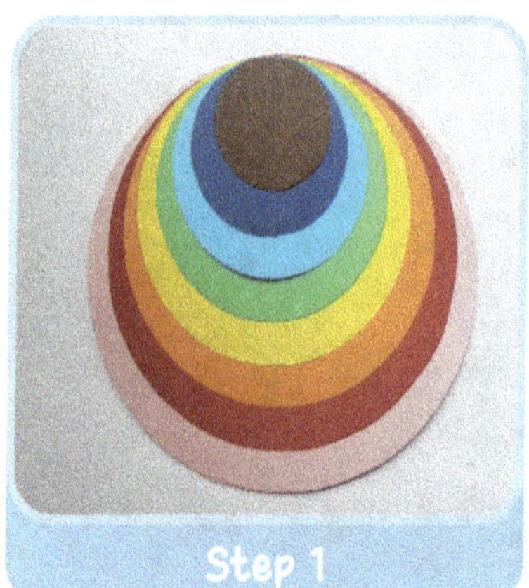

Step 1

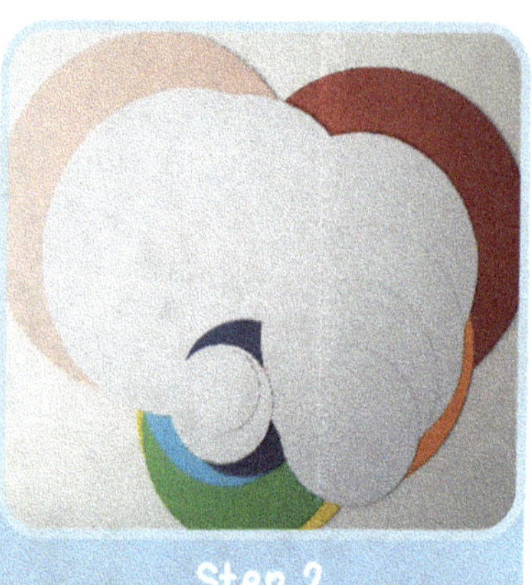

Step 2

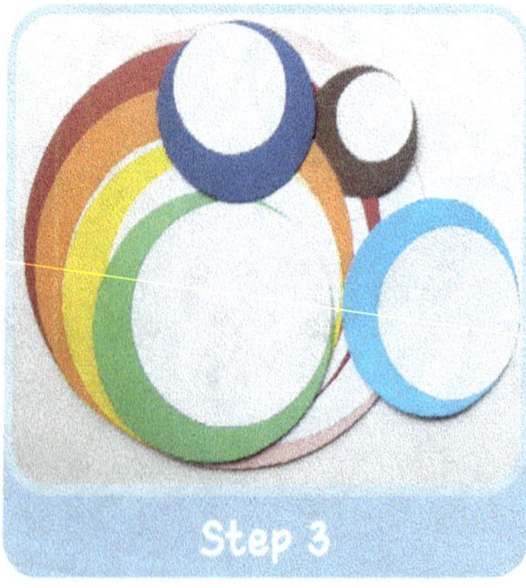

Step 3

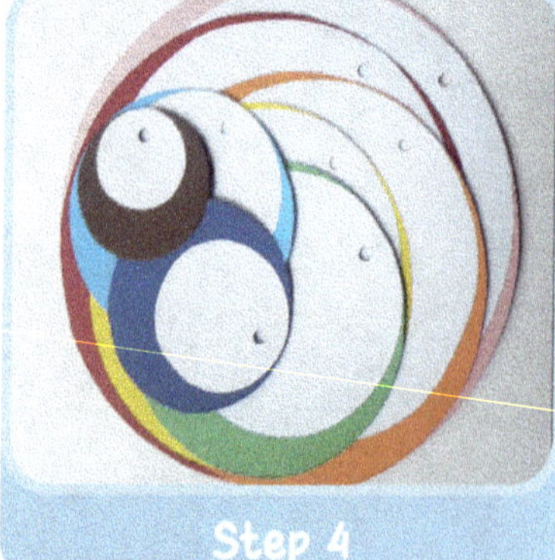

Step 4

Step 1. Cut out 8 circles, each 1" larger than the previous one and of different colors. We made them from 3" to 10".

Step 2. Cut out another 8 circles, this time all white. These circles will be glued on top of the colored circles, so they should be a little smaller. We made them from 2" to 9".

Step 3. Glue each white circle over the colored ones. Make it so that the edges of one side meet and the white part is covered by the next circle.

Step 4. Make a small hole on that side where the edges of the circles meet so that we can join them all with a ring or split pin later.

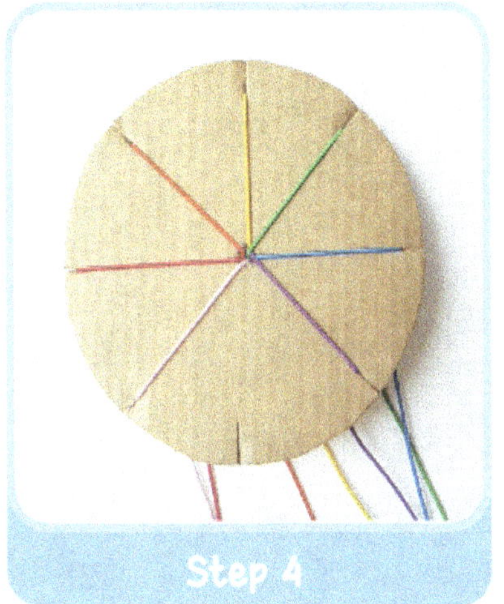

Step 4

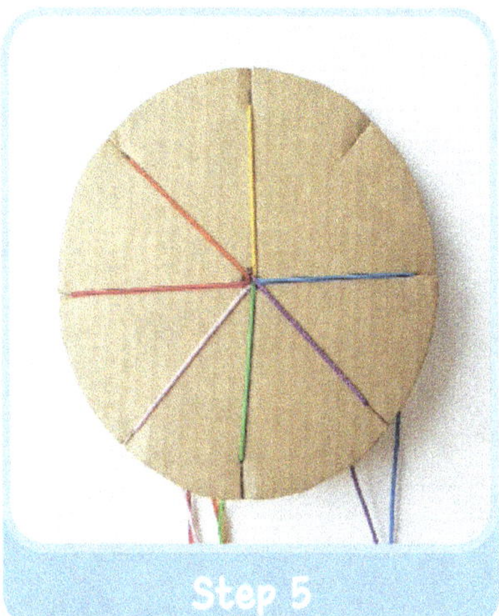

Step 5

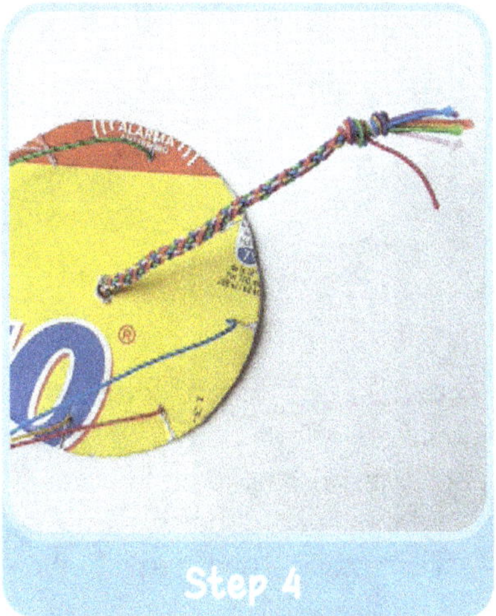

Step 4

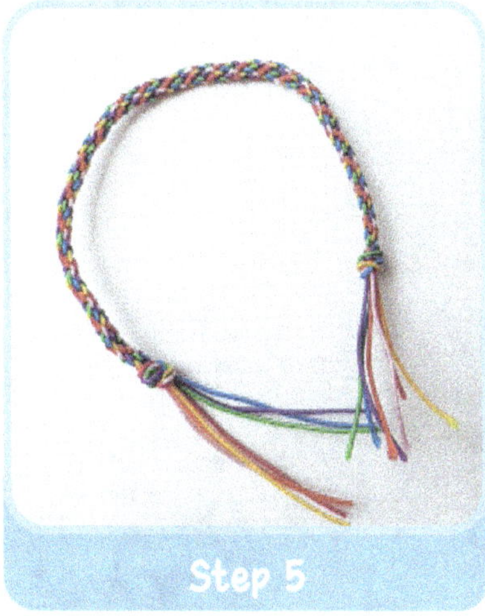

Step 5

Step 4. On the front side, insert each strand into one of the slits, leaving one of them empty. While we're making the bracelet, try to keep that empty slit at the bottom.

Step 5. With the empty slit at the bottom, count three strands to the right and move the third from its position to the empty slit. Then rotate the circle so that the new empty slit sits at the bottom.

Step 6. Repeat this process until the thread is running out and we'll see how the bracelet grows and comes out through the hole toward the back of the cardboard circle.

Step 7. Once it's the size we want, remove the bracelet from the circle, knot the end and cut the excess thread if necessary.

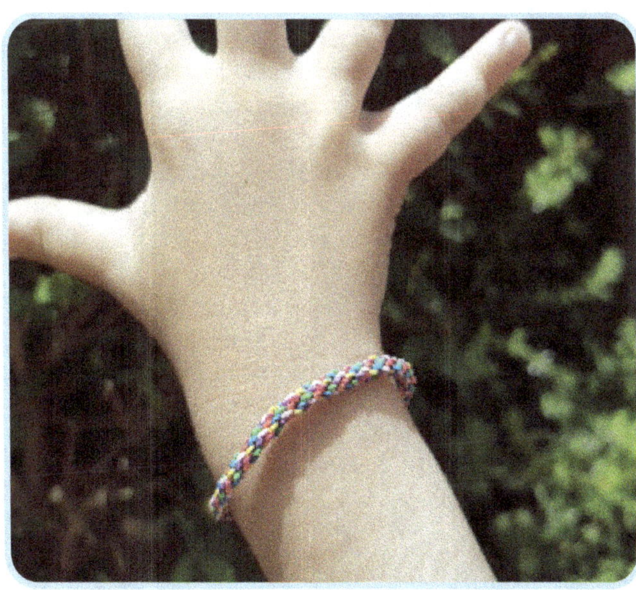

Tip: We used elastic thread to avoid having to open and close the knot when putting on and taking off the bracelet.

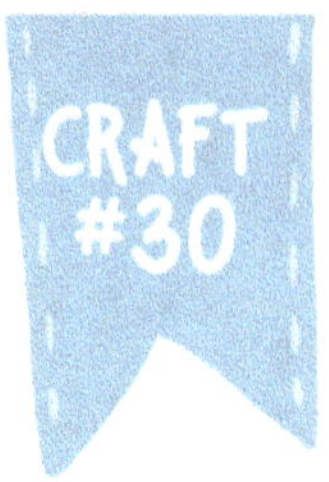

BUNNY

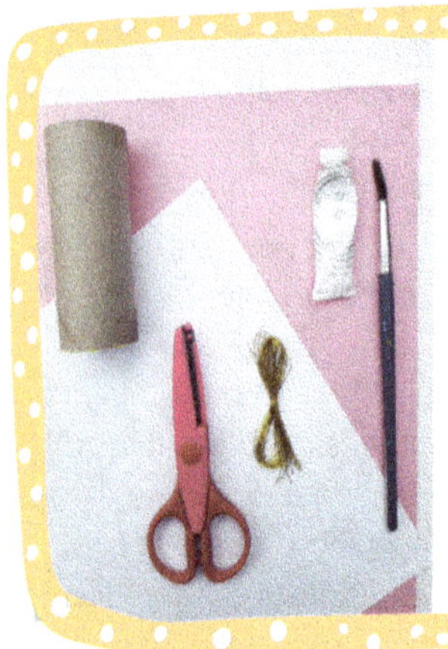

This is what we'll need:

- Toilet paper roll.
- Cardboard.
- Scissors.
- Paint and brush.
- Thread.

With Easter just around the corner, how about we make an Easter bunny that can wiggle its ears? Surely the little ones at home will have a great time with this craft!

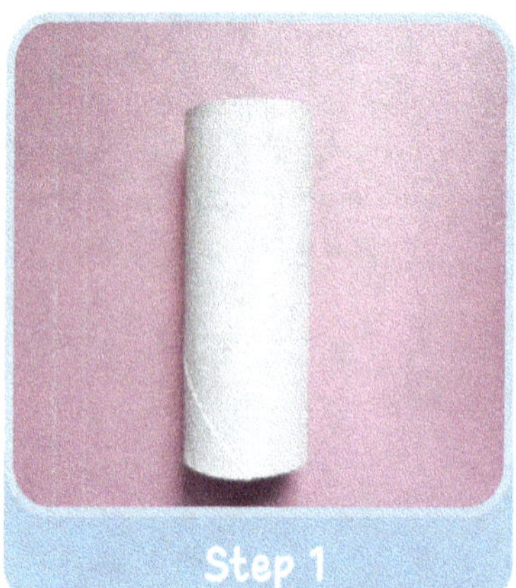

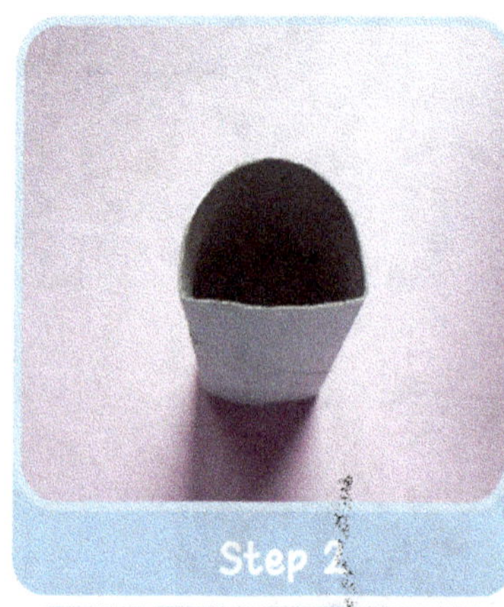

Step 1. Paint the paper roll with white paint. If we don't have white paint, another option is to cover it with white cardboard: cut out a white rectangle and glue it to the roll.

Step 2. Flatten the back of the paper roll by making a fold on each side, so that it is more or less in the shape of a semicircle.

Step 3. With white and pink cardboard, we draw and cut out the ears.

Step 4. OWith the help of scissors (or a needle if they are too big) we open three small holes in each ear. They should form a triangle with one of the holes towards the lower end of the ear and the other two a little higher.

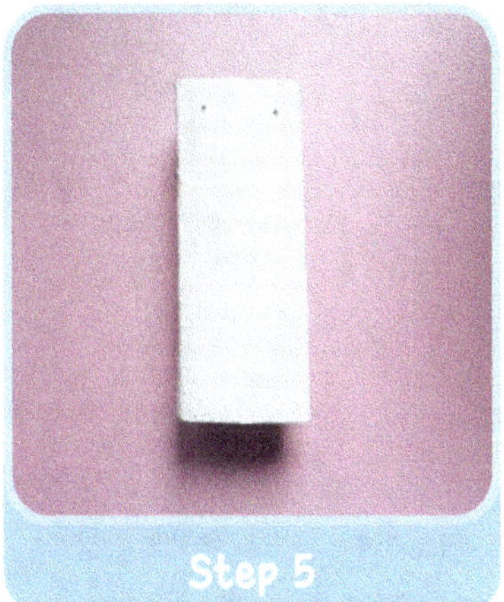

Step 5

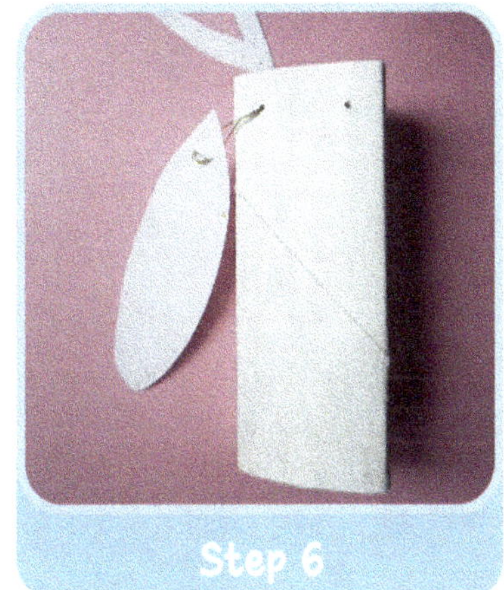

Step 6

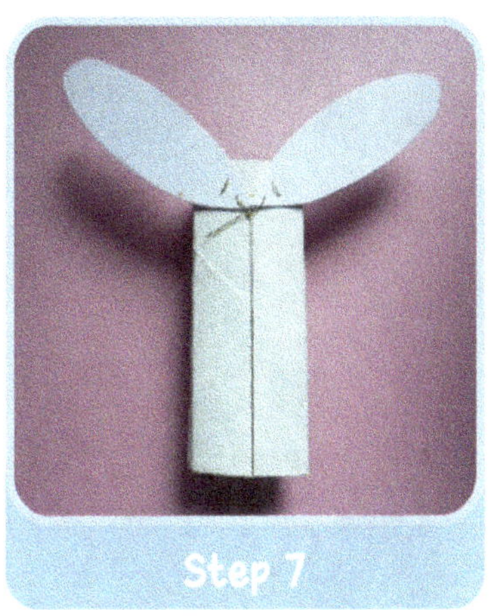

Step 7

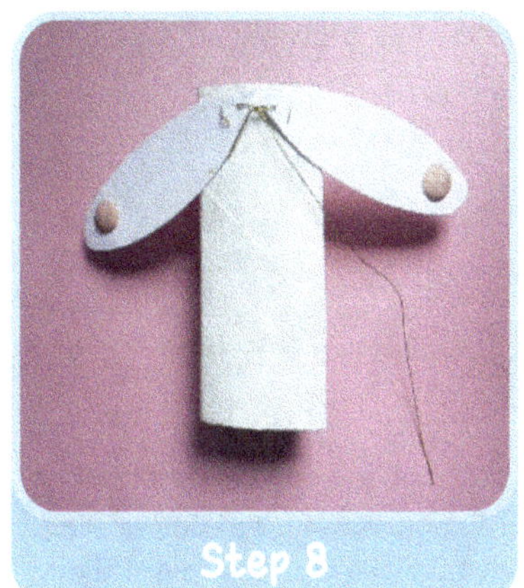

Step 8

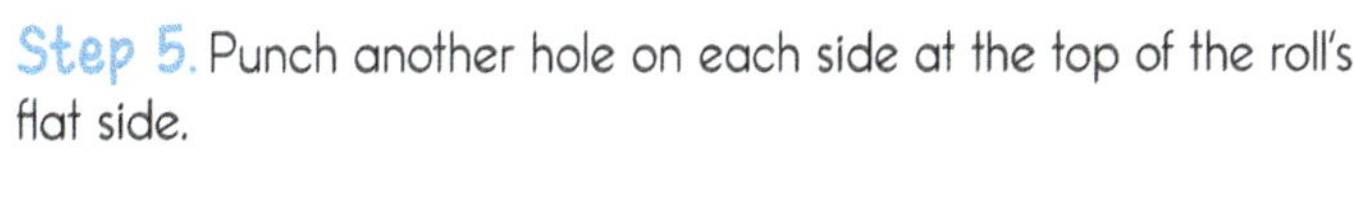

Step 5. Punch another hole on each side at the top of the roll's flat side.

Step 6. Of the three holes that we made in the ears, we put a thread through the two upper ones and introduce the two ends through one of the holes that we made in the paper roll. To keep it in place, we can tie a knot, or use adhesive tape. Repeat with the other ear.

Step 7. With another thread, we join the two holes that remain in the ears, taking into account that this thread must be long enough so that it hangs a little so we can pull it.

Step 8. We need to stick something on the back of each ear that serves as a counterweight so that they return to their initial position after moving them, such as a small piece of plasticine.

Step 9. The mechanism to move our bunny's ears is ready, now we just need to draw its face.

Tip: We can add anything we want to decorate our bunny, like an Easter egg made with wrapping paper.

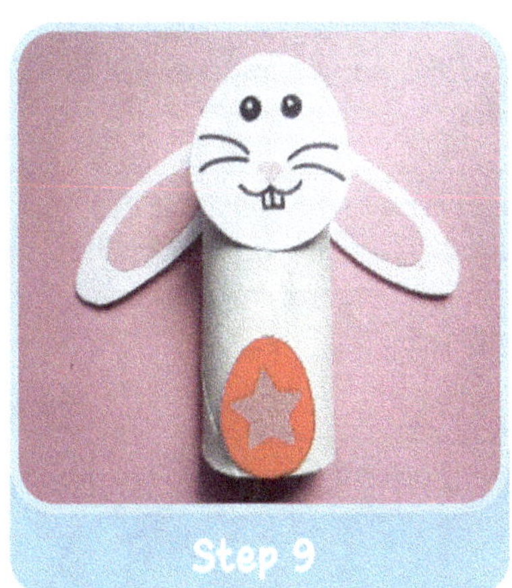

Step 9

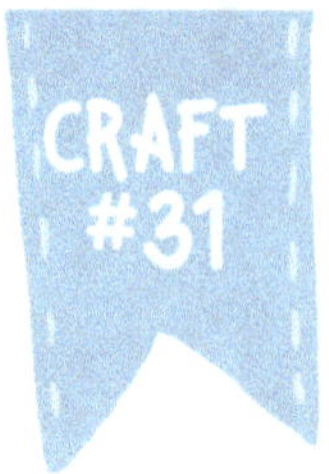

CHALK POPS

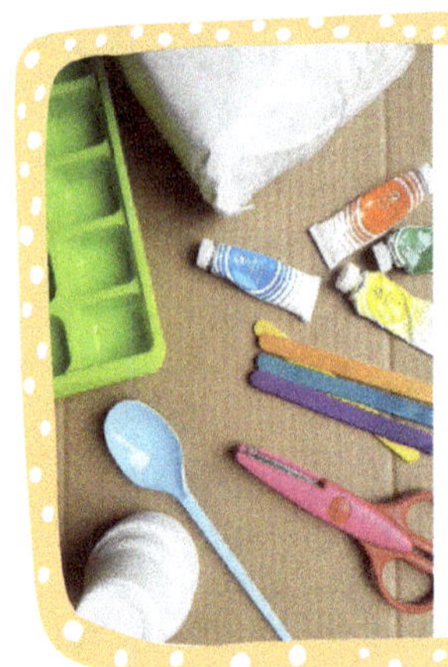

Looking for an activity to help our kids develop their creativity and get some exercise? With the chalk pops that we're going to make today they will spend hours of fun painting on the sidewalk, but they will also be able to play games like hopscotch, tic-tac-toe, and draw mazes or racetracks.

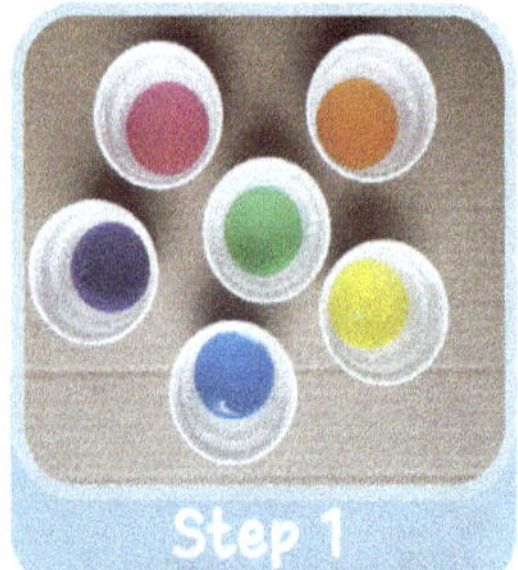

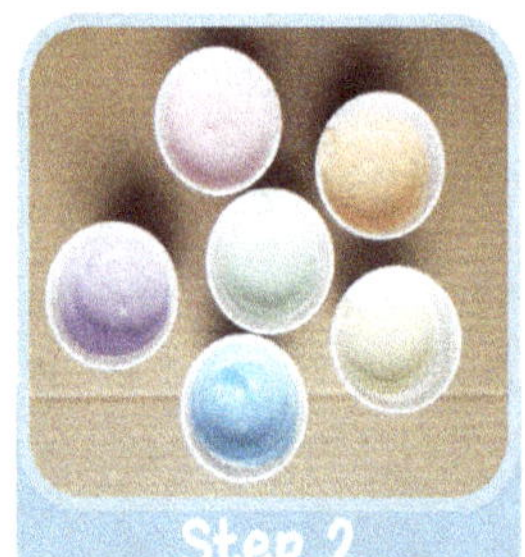

Step 1. Chill water for about half an hour before using it (it has to be cold for the plaster of Paris) and fill about 1/3 of as many cups as colors we're going to mix, then add about 2 tablespoons of tempera paint to each one. Note that the plaster of Paris should not be put down the drain, so it's best to use disposable cups to avoid having to wash them in the sink.

Step 2. Add plaster of Paris to the remaining 2/3 of each cup (I used small cups, you should adapt the amounts to your own cups and molds) and mix until everything is well combined.

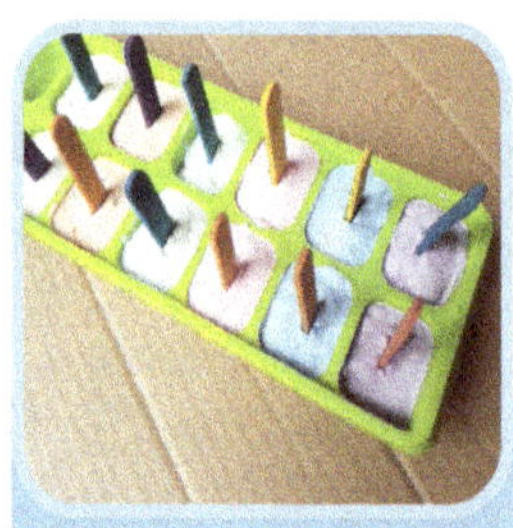

Step 3. Pour each cup into the muffin tin or ice cube tray and tap them gently against the table to remove any bubbles that may be inside.

Step 4. Wait a few minutes for the mixture to harden a bit and place half a popsicle stick in each chalk pop.

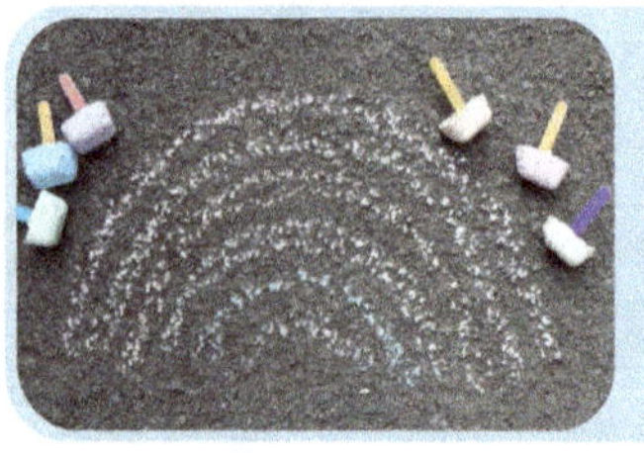

And don't worry, everything will go away later with water!

Step 5. Ideally, wait 24 hours before removing the chalk pops from the molds, although if the weather is hot enough they can be ready as soon as 4 hours. Take them out and let's draw!

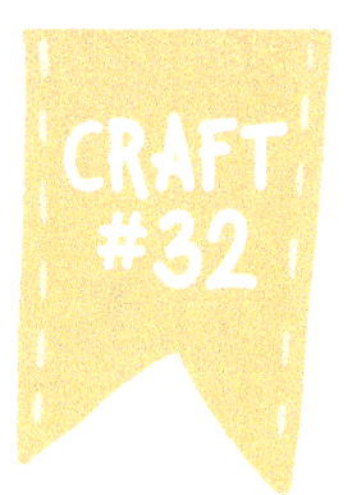

LEAF DREAM CATCHER

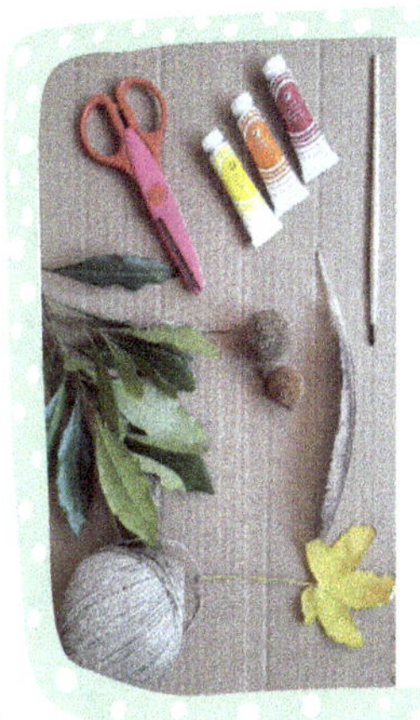

This is what we'll need:

- Paint.
- Brushes.
- Yarn.
- Scissors.
- Leaves and seeds.
- Flexible twig.

What happens if we mix a nice walk in the park or a field trip with our creativity and our kids' dreams? This craft! Ready?

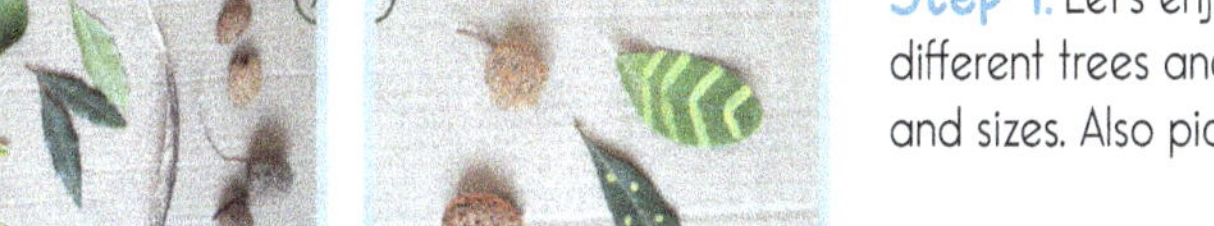
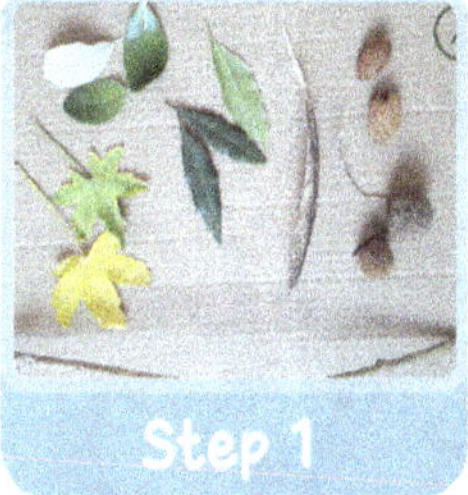
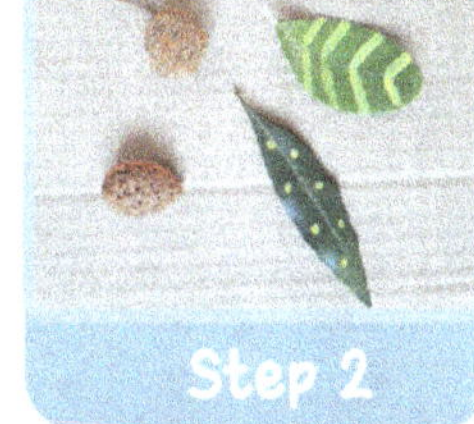

Step 1
Step 2

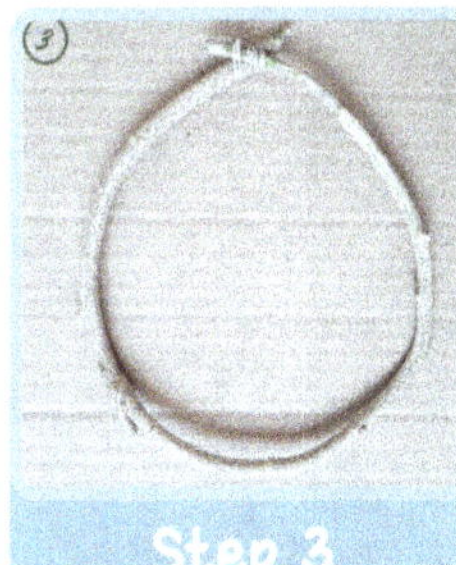

Step 3

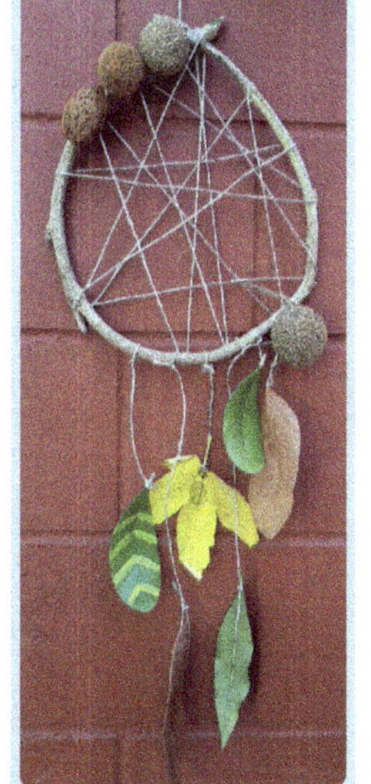

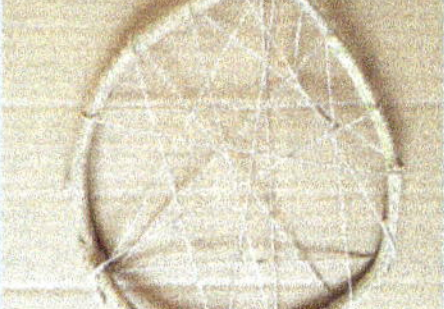

Step 4

Step 5

Step 1. Let's enjoy a day out and collect leaves and seeds from different trees and plants, as many as we want in different shapes and sizes. Also pick up a twig flexible enough to bend into a circle.

Step 2. Paint some of the leaves with stripes, dots, whatever we like, and leave some as they are. Let everything dry well.

Step 3. Bend the twig into a circle. After bending it, knot the overlapping ends with yarn so that it doesn't lose its shape. If the twig is too long, tie it to the size you want and then cut off the excess.

Step 4. Tie one end of a piece of yarn to the same place where you knotted the twig. Then take it from one side of the circle to the other at different angles each time and crossing it on itself to form the inner pattern of the dreamcatcher. We can use just one or different colors simply by knotting each piece of yarn with the next.

Step 5. Tie pieces of yarn of different sizes to the leaves that we collected and hang them from the bottom of the dream catcher. We can also glue some of them to the yarn pattern to decorate it.

Tip: We can add decorations for Halloween, Christmas, or any other special celebrations to make themed dream catchers.

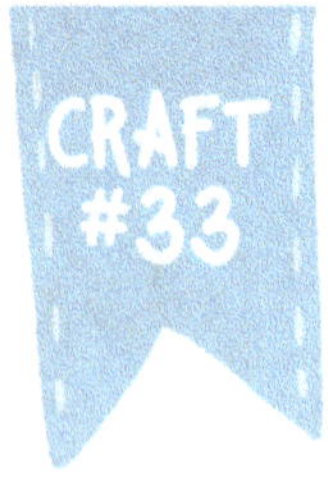

ROBOT HAND

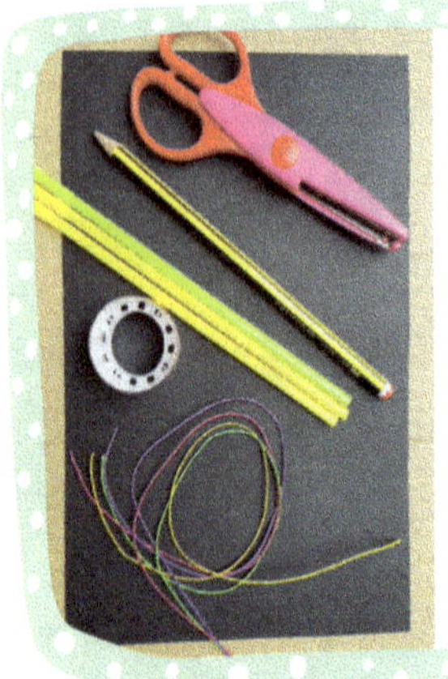

This is what we'll need:

- Cardstock.
- Tape or glue.
- Straws (regular and/or jumbo-sized).
- Yarn or twine.
- Pencil.
- Scissor.

Our hands are a somewhat complicated system because they have so many bones and muscles that allow them to move a lot and in very different ways. Today we're going to build a simple model to understand a little better how they work inside.

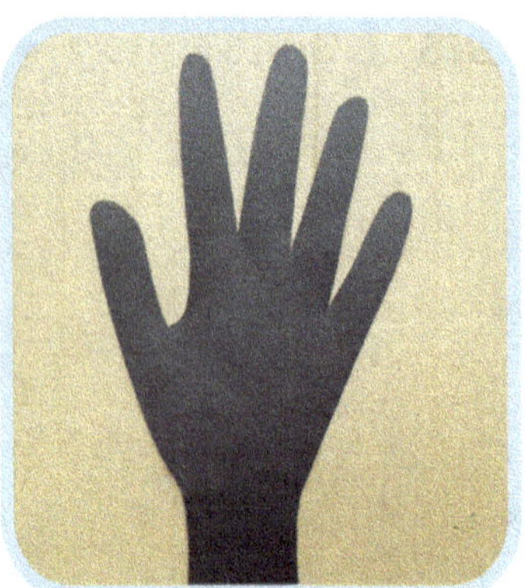

Step 1. Draw the outline of the hand and wrist on cardstock and cut it out. We can use our kid's hand, but it will be easier to put all the pieces together on a bigger hand to make it work.

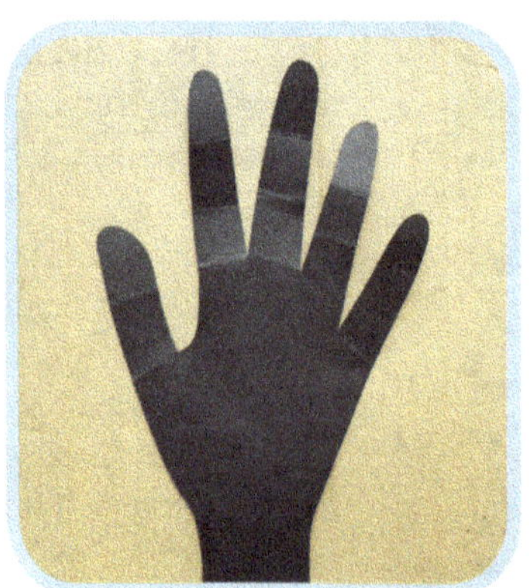

Step 2. Using our hand as a reference, mark where the finger joints are and fold the cardstock at those points. Then unfold everything.

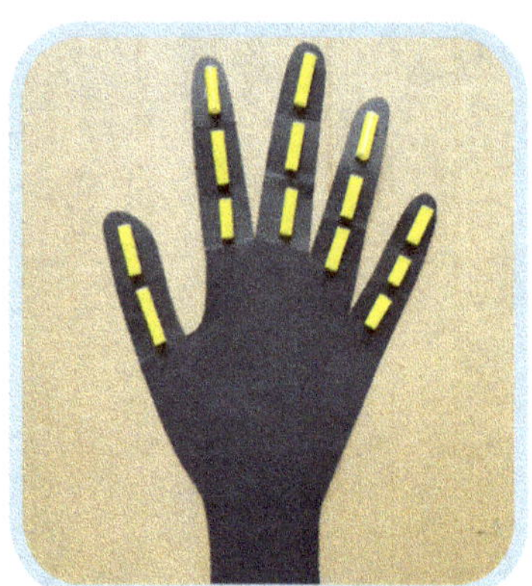

Step 3. Cut pieces of regular-sized straws to fit between the joints to make the phalanges, then glue/tape them to the fingers.

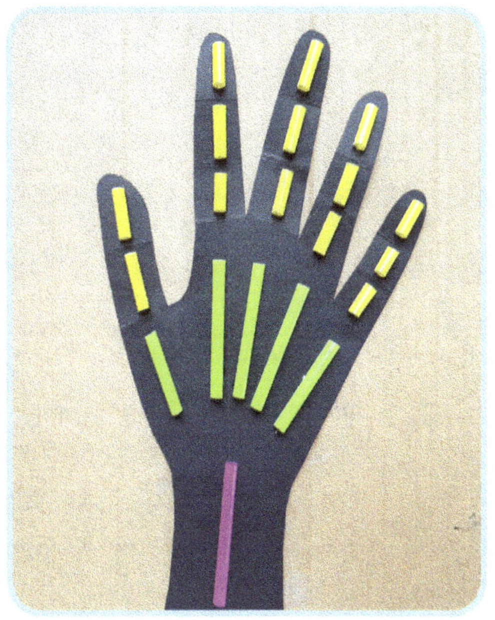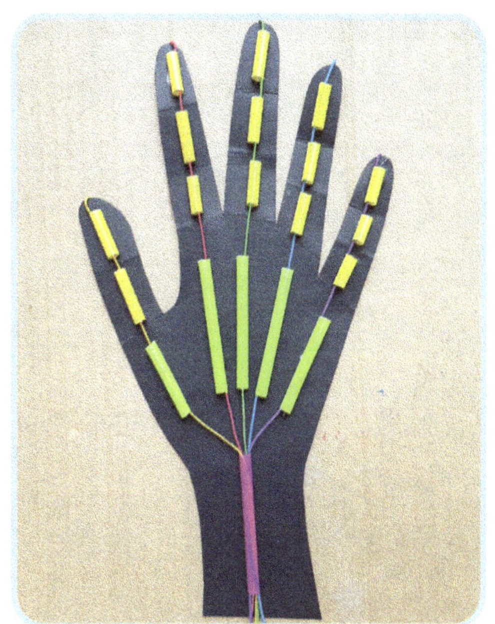

Step 4. Cut longer pieces, one per finger, and glue/tape them to the palm of the hand. Then cut another piece (we can use a jumbo-sized straw depending on the thickness of the yarn or twine we're going to use) and glue/tape it to the wrist.

Step 5. Thread a piece of yarn or twine through the straw on the wrist, then through a straw in the palm of the hand and, finally, through the phalanges of the corresponding finger. Tie a knot so it doesn't come off or glue/tape it to the tip of the finger. Repeat with the other fingers.

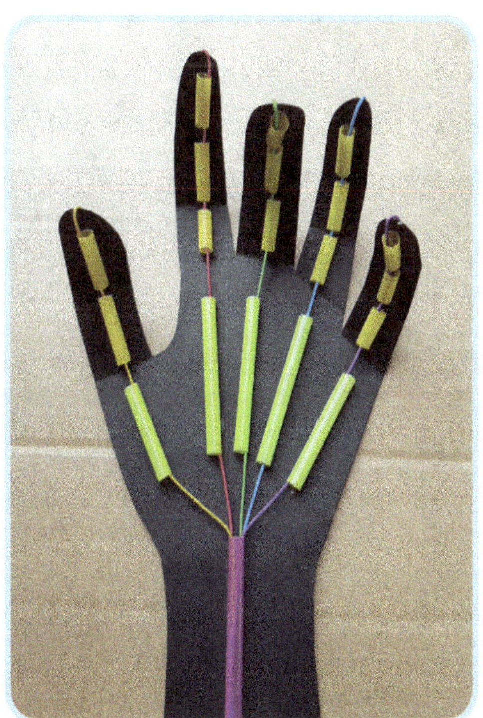

We're ready! Now we just have to pull the yarn or twine to see how the hand we just made moves.

Tip: If we use yarn or twine of different colors, it will be easier to know which one comes from each finger and we can move them independently.

SOLAR SYSTEM

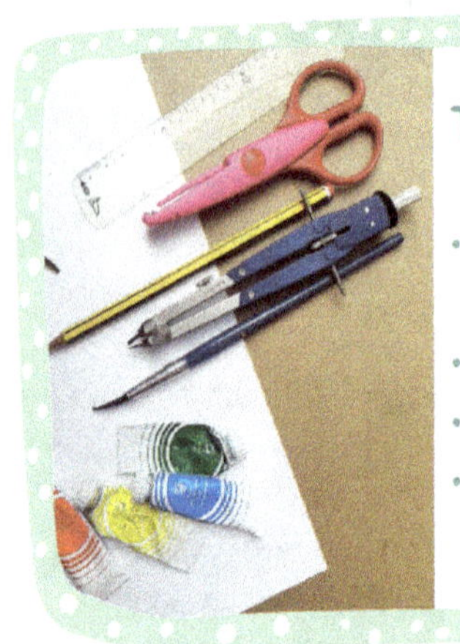

This is what we'll need:

- White paper or cardboard.
- Pencil.
- Ruler.
- Compass.
- Paint.
- Brush.
- Split pin.

A model of the Solar System is a fun way to teach our kids about the planets and how they move around the Sun. Who's up for a science project?

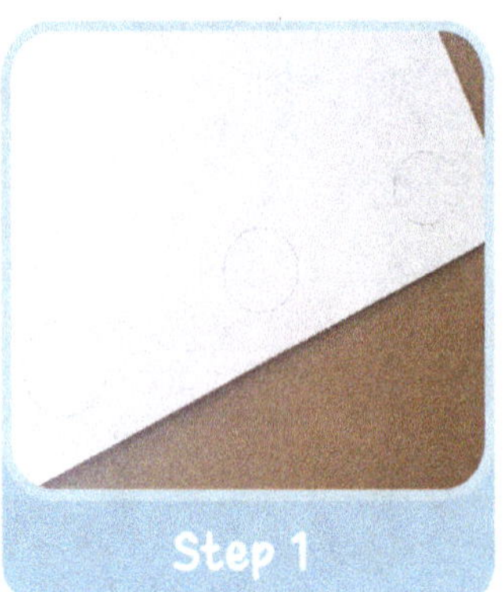

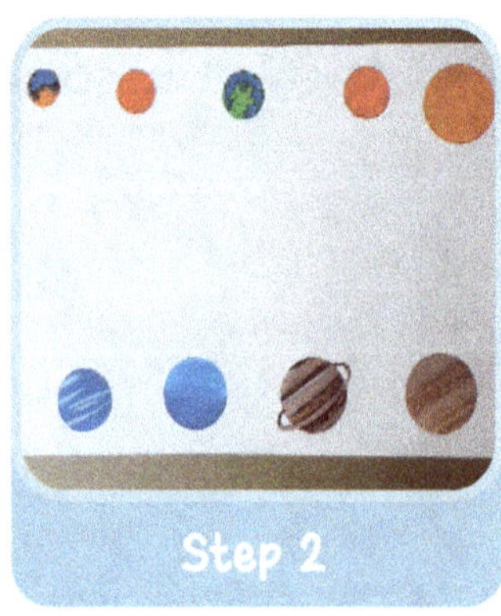

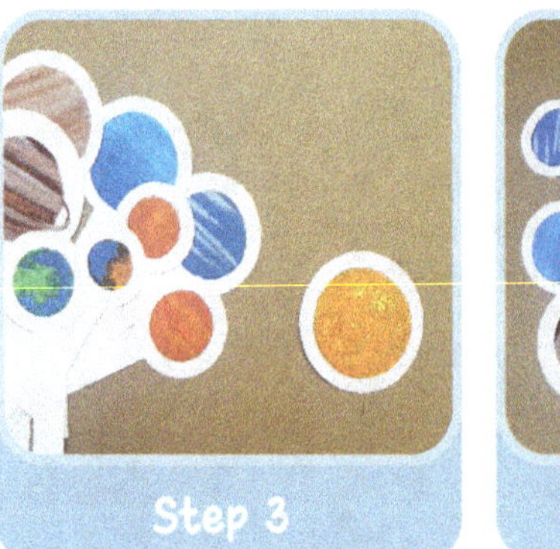

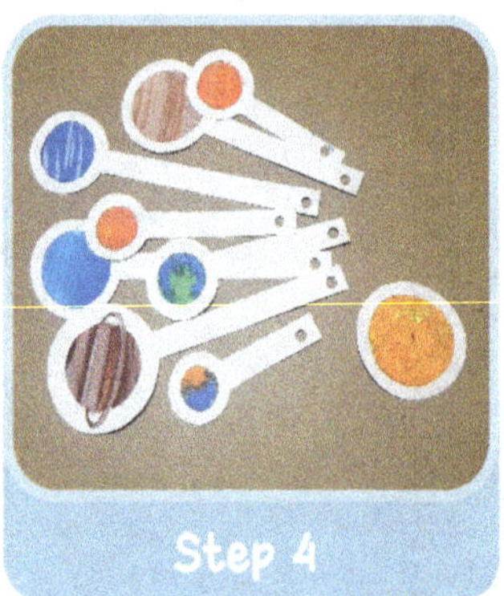

Step 1. On a piece of white cardboard or paper, draw 9 circles, each one larger than the previous one. These will be the Sun and the 8 planets. We can use coins or bottle caps if we don't have a compass.

Step 2. Color each planet and the Sun with their corresponding colors. From smallest to largest they are: Mercury, Mars, Venus, Earth, Neptune, Uranus, Saturn, Jupiter, and the Sun. Don't forget the rings of Saturn!

Step 3. Cut out each planet leaving a white margin of about 0.5". On one side, it doesn't matter which one, leave a rectangle 0.5" wide. Its length will depend on the planet: Mercury 2", Venus 2.5", Earth 3", Mars 3.5", Jupiter 4", Saturn 4.5", Uranus 5", and Neptune 5.5".

Step 4. Cut out the Sun, also leaving a 0.5" edge, but in this case we're not cutting out any rectangles.

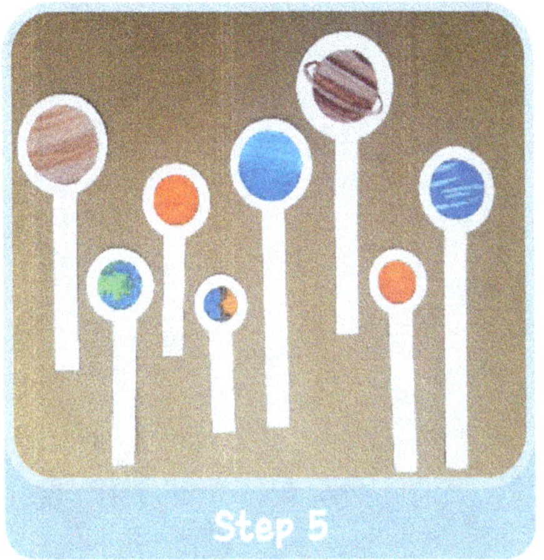

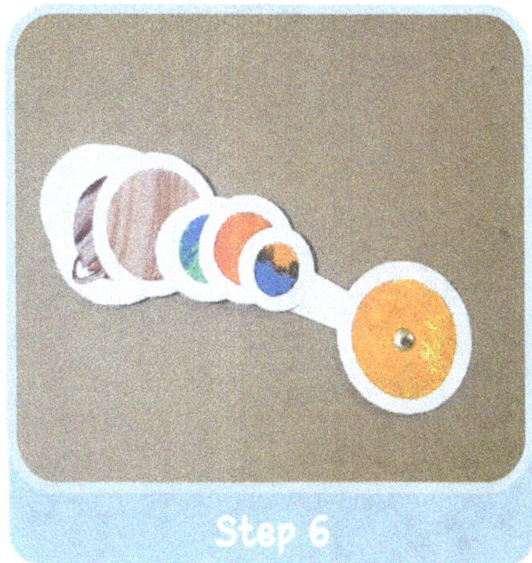

Step 5. Make a small hole with the tip of the scissors (or a puncher) at the end of each planet's rectangle and a slot in the center of the Sun, being careful not to tear the paper.

Step 6. Arrange the planets from closest to furthest from the Sun (rectangles from shortest to longest), matching the holes at the ends. Place the Sun on top and connect them all with a split pin.

Step 7. Move the planets sideways so they don't overlap and so they look like they are orbiting the Sun.

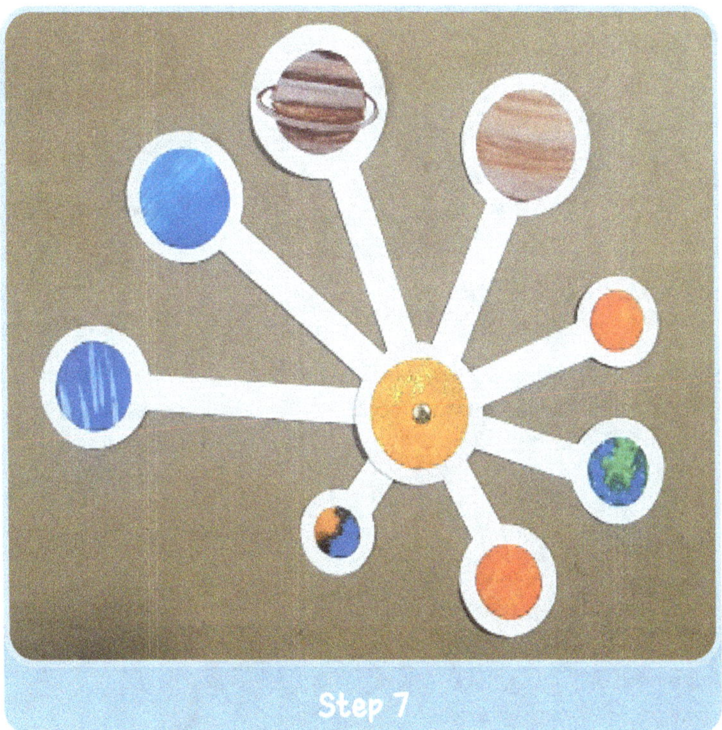

Tip: If we use paper instead of cardboard and it's not strong enough, we can stick a toothpick, skewer or popsicle stick on the bottom so that the planets remain straight. We can also use the rectangles to write each planet's name.

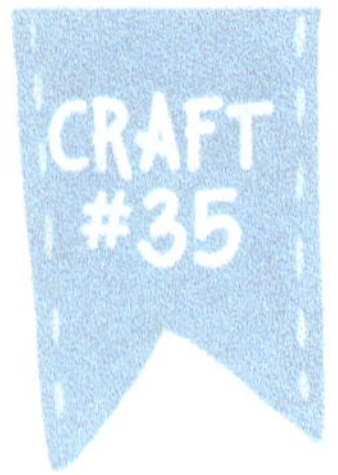

PYRAMID PUZZLE

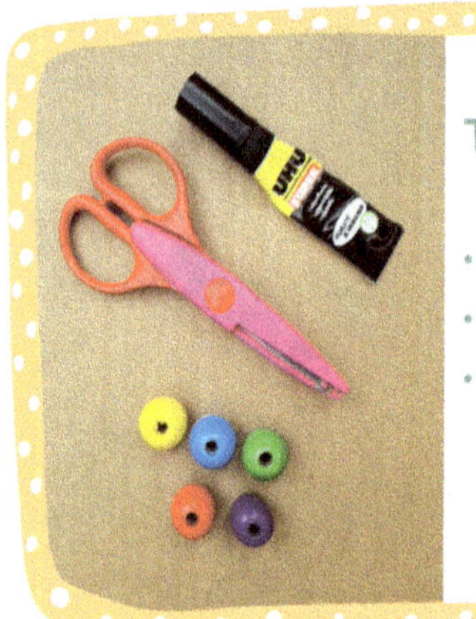

This is what we'll need:

- Wooden beads.
- Glue.
- Optional: cardboard and scissors.

Have you ever heard of the sphere pyramid puzzle? It's a pyramid made with wooden beads that form pieces of 2, 3, or 4 beads glued together. It's really easy to make and a lot of fun to solve, and it also challenges our kids' spatial vision and problem-solving skills (and ours too!).

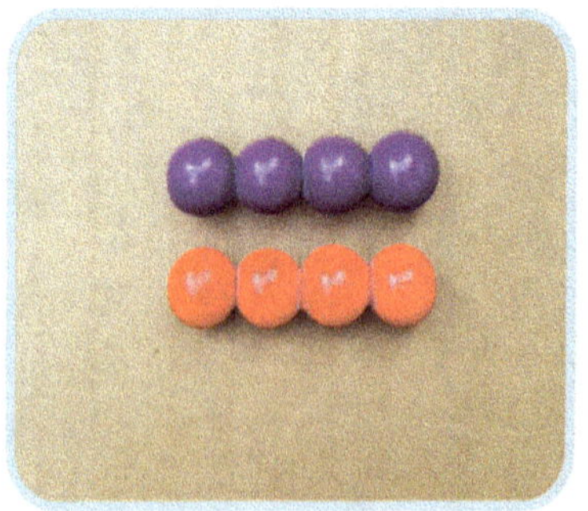

Step 1. Glue 4 wooden beads together to form a line. Repeat with 4 other beads to get 2 pieces of 4 beads each.

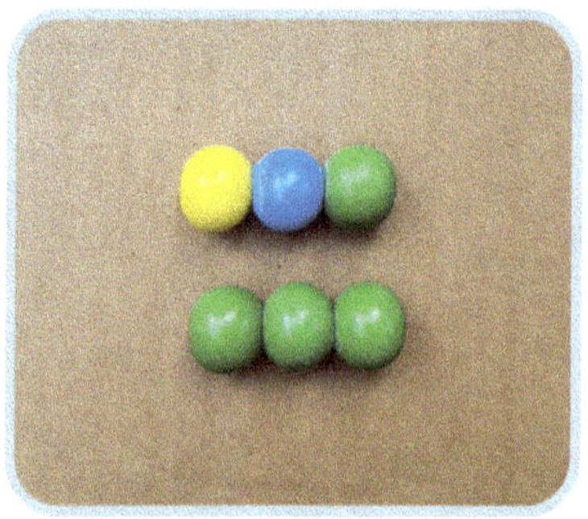

Step 2. Do the same to get 2 pieces of 3 beads each.

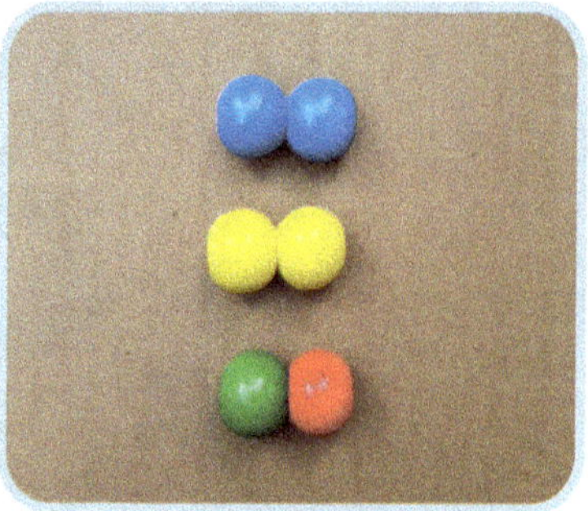

Step 3. Repeat the same process to get 3 pieces of 2 beads each.

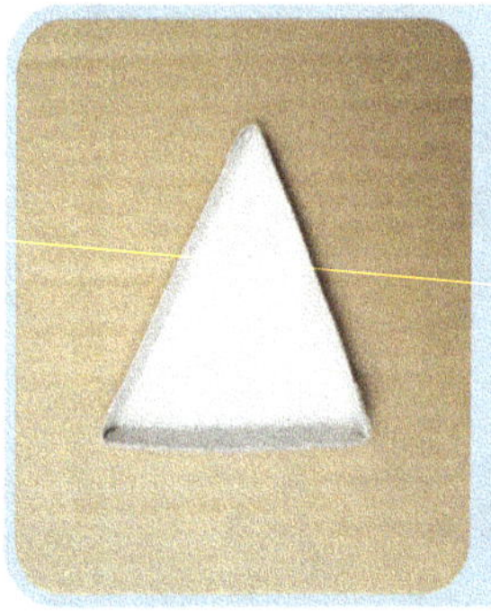

Tip: Use cardboard to cut out a triangle the same size as the pyramid. It's going to be the base of our pyramid, so it's important that it has small 'walls' to keep the pieces in place.

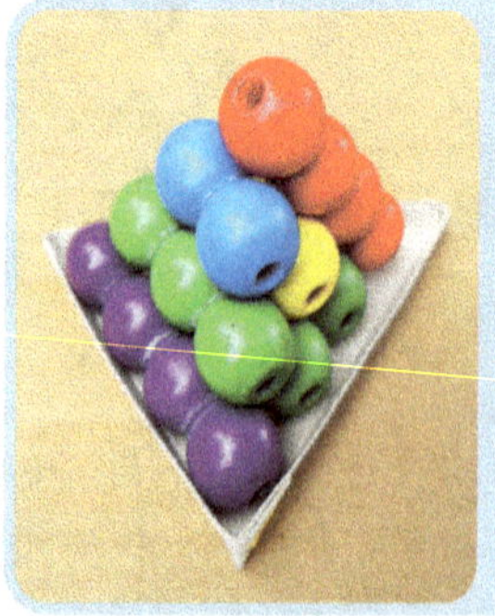

How to play: Try to build a 3D pyramid by placing the pieces on top of each other, keeping in mind that we have to use all of them.